Stress Relief That Works

ALSO BY KALINDA ROSE STEVENSON

STRESS RELIEF
THAT WORKS

How To
Think Your Way
From Stressed-Out to Peaceful

Kalinda Rose Stevenson, Ph.D.

ABKA

ABKA Publishing

Published by ABKA Publishing, Las Vegas, Nevada.

ISBN-13: 978-0692463307
ISBN-10: 0692463305

Cover design by Kalinda Rose Stevenson and James L. Stevenson.

This publication is designed to provide accurate and authoritative information in regard to the subject matter covered. It is sold with the understanding that the publisher is not engaged in rendering legal, accounting, or other professional services. If legal advice or other expert assistance is required, the services of a competent professional person should be sought.

Library of Congress Control Number: 2015943087

It's not the situation that's causing your stress, it's your thoughts, and you can change that right here and now. You can choose to be peaceful right here and now. Peace is a choice, and it has nothing to do with what other people do or think.

Gerald Jampolsky

Free Thank You Bonus

THE COMPANION QUESTION BOOK FOR STRESS RELIEF THAT WORKS

Each chapter in *Stress Relief That Works: How to Think Your Way from Stressed-Out to Peaceful* ends with some questions to help you think about stress in your life.

The Companion Question Book for *Stress Relief That Works* is a free downloadable PDF. It includes all of these questions in one place with some space to answer the questions and make notes.

The purpose of the questions is to encourage you to do more than read the book, but also to take the next step and write down your thoughts about these questions. Writing gets the thoughts out of your head so that you can look at what and how you think about stress in your life.

You can find the download link to the free bonus in Resources.

Contents

Free Thank You Bonus   iv

PART I   THINKING ABOUT STRESSORS AND STRESS

Chapter 1   Thinking Your Way From Stressed-Out to Peaceful   9

Chapter 2   Thinking About Stress   23

Chapter 3   Thinking About Stress and Thought   31

PART II   THINKING ABOUT WHAT YOU SAY ABOUT STRESS

Chapter 4   Thinking About Stress and Speech   45

Chapter 5   Thinking About Stress and Vision   55

Chapter 6   Thinking About Stress and Perspective   67

PART III   THINKING ABOUT STRESSORS AND TIME

Chapter 7   Thinking About Stress and Time   77

Chapter 8   Thinking About Stress and Enough   89

Chapter 9   Thinking About Stress and Your Past   103

Chapter 10   Thinking About Stress and Your Future   117

PART IV   THINKING ABOUT STRESS AND YOUR SELF

Chapter 11   Thinking About Your Self-Image   129

Chapter 12   Thinking About Your Self-Esteem   139

Chapter 13   Thinking About Your Self-Trust   149

PART V   THINKING ABOUT RE-CREATING YOUR SELF

Chapter 14   Thinking About Re-Creating Your Self   165

Chapter 15   Thinking About The Language of Creation   179

Chapter 16   Thinking About Energy   191

PART VI   THINKING ABOUT YOUR PEACEFUL LIFE

Chapter 17   Thinking About Serenity   205

Chapter 18   Thinking About Grace   215

Chapter 19   Thinking About Your Life Journey   227

About the Author   237

Write a Review   238

Resources   239

Notes   241

Index   245

PART I

THINKING ABOUT STRESSORS AND STRESS

Chapter 1

Thinking Your Way
From Stressed-Out to Peaceful

Most of us are operating in a state of chronic stress;
we're always on.

David W. Ballard

STRESSED-OUT

Do you feel *stressed-out* much of the time? If you do, you're not alone. Feeling stressed-out has become the dominant way of life for many of us. Although *stress* is a fact of life in our world, definitions of stress cover such a wide range of meanings that any reference to stress is ambiguous. Stress can refer to a cause or an effect. Stress can be good. Stress can be bad. However, the description *stressed-out* is clear. Stressed-out refers to a way of life.

It's also essential to make a clear distinction between two types of stress. The first type of stress concerns external threats and potential catastrophes, such as wars, life-threatening weather conditions, dangerous people, and traumatic experiences. This is *traumatic stress,* caused by terrifying circumstances, with life-changing impact.

The second type of stress concerns responsibilities in your daily life, such as personal relationships and conflicts, health problems, financial struggles, jobs, housework, home maintenance, paying bills, buying food, fixing meals, doing laundry, taking care of children, driving on busy roads. This is *chronic stress*. Chronic stress produces stressed-out lives.

This book focuses on chronic stress. If you feel stressed-out most of the time by the ordinary stresses of daily life, feeling stressed-out has become a way of life. The good news is that you can change stressed-out to peaceful by how you think.

ALWAYS ON

Ponder David Ballard's claim that most of us are operating in a state of chronic stress and are always "on." Certainly, life on Earth is no picnic. As long as human beings have existed, our species has experienced every type of stress imaginable, endured every kind of catastrophe, every kind of climate, including ice ages, engaged in horrendous wars, killed wild animals or were killed by them, endured the hardships and struggles of finding shelter, food, and water, and the pains, sufferings, and sorrows of childbirth, illness, injuries, and death.

Now, most of us in the western world live in buildings with hot and cold running water, indoor plumbing, electricity, central heat, air conditioning, stoves, microwaves, refrigerators, TVs, computers, internet access, cell phones, and iPads—to name a few of the "essentials" of contemporary life our not-so-distant ancestors couldn't have imagined. We buy food in supermarkets stocked with an abundance of food—some of it real and much of it not so real—including exotic food from around the world that has become ordinary and available almost anywhere at almost any time of the year. Meanwhile, we travel the world in automobiles, trains, airplanes, and ships, while orbiting satellites allow us to communicate with almost anyone anywhere in the world in a matter of seconds. No generation of people on Earth ever had so much.

So why is it, in the beginning years of the twenty-first century, when we have more available to us than any other people in the long history of Earth, why are we so stressed-out? If we're always "on," who turned us on? How do we find the *Stressed-Out Off Switch?*

CREATING YOUR STRESSED-OUT OFF SWITCH

You'll find various methods for relieving chronic stress. Many stress relief methods treat stress as a condition you "manage" or "relieve" or "reduce" by methods such as meditation or relaxation or deep breathing or exercise to tame the unwelcome bully in your life called "stress." Although these treatment methods are valuable and worth making part of your life, they don't address the primary cause of chronic stress.

Your ability to create your own Stressed-Out Off Switch begins with a significant distinction:

Stress is a reaction to a stressor.

Although we'll come back to specific definitions of *stress* and *stressor* in Chapter 1, simply recognizing this distinction leads to a profoundly liberating insight:

You are not at the mercy of some unwanted oppressor called "stress."

A famous Pogo cartoon by Walt Kelly had this memorable phrase:

We have met the enemy and he is us.[1]

These words from an old cartoon focus on the primary creator of your stressed-out feelings—you. You create your experience of stress by your reactions to stressors in your life. You can point to all of the reasons why you are feeling stressed-out. Your job. The people in your life. Money. The economy. All of those items can be powerful stressors, but the real culprit who causes your stress is you. Although this might sound harsh and unsympathetic, the good news in this claim is that you aren't a helpless victim of some external force called Stress. Stressors have been with us always and will be with us always. However, living in a perpetually stressed-out state of mind and body is NOT inevitable.

If you recognize your own chronically stressed-out life as your reaction to stressors, you can also recognize that "stressed-out" becomes something you do to yourself. This doesn't mean that you *cause* the stressors. It does mean that you can *choose* how you react to stressors in your life. Why is this good news? As the creator of your stressed-out state of mind, you can't *find* a Stressed-Out Off Switch outside yourself, but you can *create* your own Stressed-Out Off Switch.

YOUR THOUGHTS AND YOUR STRESS

Consider Gerald Jampolsky's claim:

> It's not the situation that's causing your stress, it's your thoughts, and you can change that right here and now. You can choose to be peaceful right here and now. Peace is a choice, and it has nothing to do with what other people do or think.

Jampolsky refers to "the situation that's causing your stress." The situation is the stressor. He then claims that your thoughts cause your stress. This means you can change your life from stressed-out to peaceful by *how and what you think about stress and stressors* in your life.

The corollary of this claim is that *how and what you think about stress and stressors depends on the words you use.* Thoughts and words are inseparable. Although many self-help teachers claim that the mind "thinks" in pictures rather than words, *thinking* involves specific words. When you see images in your mind, you very quickly define what you see with words. Even if you say that the image you see is "indescribable," you're using a word to describe what you see.

The simple truth is that you—and only you—have power over your words. You don't always choose your life experiences, but you can always choose the words you use. A powerful way to think about stress and stressors in your stressed-out life is to investigate your words.

Think about the importance of words in your life. The words you say. The words you hear. The words you read. The words you write. Think especially about the words you think. You visualize in pictures, but you think in words. Your ability to turn *feeling stressed-out* into *feeling peaceful* begins by recognizing the power of the words you think to create your stressed-out feelings.

YOUR WORDS AND YOUR STRESS

Before you consider the stressors in your life, consider what happens to you when you describe yourself as "stressed-out." Emotions—feelings—are sensations within you. As soon as you describe your feelings, you're using words. It's a short distance between *feeling* an emotion, to *naming* the emotion, to having the words *name* you. Who are you? You are *Stressed-Out*.

Can you really turn *stressed-out* into peaceful by changing your words? Yes, you can. Whatever other skills you possess, whatever your life circumstances, whether you're struggling for money, whether you feel stuck in some place you don't want to be, whoever the people are in your life, you can change how you think about stressors and stress in your life by changing the words you use.

You can choose to become aware of what you say out loud and what you say to yourself in that that constant running commentary that goes on in your head. You can decide to empower yourself with your words and eliminate the words that rob you of power. However people talk around you, or about you, or to you, you don't have to be bound by anyone else's words. Even when you're not free to speak words of power out loud, you can use whatever words you choose to create your thoughts.

WHY DOESN'T SOMEBODY DO SOMETHING?

For a demonstration of how thoughts and words create the experience of feeling stressed-out, think about a young man at a San Francisco fireworks display one Fourth of July. Each year, San

Francisco puts on a spectacular fireworks display over San Francisco Bay. One of the realities of going to fireworks displays in San Francisco on the Fourth of July is that San Francisco can be a very cold and foggy place in summer.

The annual fireworks display is a demonstration of hope that the fog will stay beyond the Golden Gate long enough for the four hundred thousand people gathered to see the fireworks shot off from barges in Marina Park and San Francisco Bay. Some years it does. Some years it doesn't. This was one of those years when the statement incorrectly attributed to Mark Twain makes perfect sense: "The coldest winter I ever spent was a summer in San Francisco."

On this particular Fourth of July, the cold fog rolled in before the fireworks. My husband and I huddled on a pier in the Embarcadero that was crammed with other hopefuls who were waiting for the fireworks. A group of six friends in their early twenties stood beside us. When the time came to fire off the display, the sky was filled with dense fog. In San Francisco on the Fourth of July, thick fog is no reason to cancel the fireworks. The fireworks lit up the clouds with a surreal display of colors

One of the young men in the group beside us was upset. He described his unhappiness in an ongoing stream of outraged words: "Why doesn't somebody do something about this?" As the barrage of fireworks continued, he became more and more upset. He complained on and on as his outrage grew more intense: "Why are they doing this? Why don't they fix it? Why doesn't somebody DO something?"

His friends remained silent. It's reasonable to assume that they were disappointed too, but they didn't complain endlessly. It's also reasonable to assume that multitude of people huddled in the cold fog that San Francisco Fourth of July were also disappointed, but I suspect that most didn't keep complaining in outrage that someone needed to do something about the fog.

This unhappy young man demonstrates how stress can be self-created by thoughts. He became increasingly stressed-out by a weather condition that no one could control. He was old enough to understand that fog can't be controlled by mere humans on barges on the San Francisco Bay. And yet, he ranted on and on about how someone should do something to fix what was not fixable.

HOW TO CREATE STRESS IN YOUR LIFE

This story demonstrates how you can create stress in your life. This example of self-induced stress might seem like an extreme case, but it isn't. Something unwanted happens. You feel powerless to stop it, control it, or change it. How do you react? Do you drive yourself deeper and deeper into a stressed-out state? Or do you recognize that you can control how you react by how you think about it?

The young man was powerless to change the circumstances. So were the rest of the four hundred thousand people gathered along the waterfront. Becoming stressed-out was a matter of individual response. The young man got very upset. Perhaps others also got equally upset. I suspect that most people took it as the way things are. Maybe young children don't know any better, but the rest of us do. The fog is not something you can control.

Unwanted circumstances are inevitable facts of life. You might not stress out over fireworks being shot into the fog. The question is:

how often do you become stressed-out by unwanted occurrences that are no one's fault and no one can fix?

The worst part of the story for the young man is that he robbed himself of a unique experience. As a lifelong lover of fireworks, I can tell you that I had never experienced a fireworks display like that. Although no familiar patterns lit up the sky, the fireworks turned the fog into a dazzling display of exquisite colors. The clouds overhead became a lightshow of fantastic swirling textures and colors. I loved it. That experience has nothing to with what might have been on a clear night. Rather the fireworks in the fog became a memory I'll never forget.

Unexpected, unwanted circumstances can become extraordinary experiences. The old adage proclaims: "If life hands you lemons, make lemonade." You always have a choice about how you react to what happens to you. Choosing "stressed-out" is one option. You always have the choice to think your way to a better option.

Choosing to Be Peaceful

The second part of Jampolsky's quotation identifies a better option. You can choose to be peaceful:

> You can choose to be peaceful right here and now. Peace is a choice, and it has nothing to do with what other people do or think.

The opposite of stressed-out is peaceful. Rather than harried and hurried, you feel calm and serene. The essential difference between stressed-out and peaceful is not a matter of *doing*, it's a matter of *thinking*. Both stressed-out and peaceful are states of mind. Your state of mind determines how you perceive your life and the outside world. Your state of mind defines your perspective on life, your attitude, and your mood. Most significantly, your state of mind defines your perception of yourself.

Gerald Jampolsky's words about stress lay out clearly the central claim of this book: how you *think* about stress in your life makes the difference between stressed-out and peaceful:

> It's not the situation that's causing your stress, it's your thoughts, and you can change that right here and now. You can choose to be peaceful right here and now. Peace is a choice, and it has nothing to do with what other people do or think.

PERSPECTIVES ON STRESS

At the same time, the last sentence oversimplifies the role of other people and external circumstances in producing stress in your life because it ignores context. It also ignores the difference between traumatic stress and chronic stress. It's easy to make simplistic one-size-fits-all statements about stress in your life. One-size-fits-all of anything might fit many people, but not everyone.

I've cited many insightful quotations about stress in this book. They're included because each offers a valuable perspective on some aspect of stress. At the same time, each statement is only one perspective on the complicated topic of stress. Perspective describes what you see and think when you view something from a specific location. What you see or don't see is limited by location, focus, unique experience, and vision. A single perspective can never see the whole of anything,

A statement such as "Peace is a choice, and it has nothing to do with what other people do or think" needs to be qualified based on context and who has power to hurt you. Feeling stressed-out by day-to-day routines in an affluent first world society is one thing. If you realize that your thoughts are causing your stressed-out feelings, you're free *to think about how you think* about stressors in your life. You can also choose peaceful rather than stressed-out as a way of life.

However, feeling stressed-out because you're afraid for your life in some dangerous context is another matter. If you're feeling stressed-out because you're in a life-threatening situation, you need more than simple statements about changing your mindset. In addition to thinking about how you think about stressors, you also need a way out of your unsafe situation. Although finding wise, competent, and compassionate sources of help can be a challenge, I urge you to seek help. You deserve a better life.

CREATING A PEACEFUL LIFE

I assume that most people who read a book about stress have some combination of the two types of stress experiences. No one goes through life unscathed by traumatic and painful experiences. At the same time, rapid change in our world swamps us with more and more and more of everything at an ever-increasing pace. The world is moving at a rate that is too fast for anyone to keep up.

How can you free yourself from a painful past, live in a fast-paced world of constant change, and create a peaceful life? You begin by paying attention to how you think about stress in your life. Celebrate your moments of awareness. They serve you well. They enable you to see beyond the idea of taming or managing or controlling some unwanted entity called "Stress." Transforming stressed-out into peaceful is a process, not a magic formula. Words of wisdom—such as Gerald Jampolsky's statement about stress—are not the whole truth, but they can guide you well.

Whatever your current life situation—whether you feel stressed-out because of too much to do and not enough time to do it or you're afraid for your life—resolve to treat yourself and others with compassion. Whatever you do, don't fall into the trap of judging yourself harshly when you discover that you're thinking your way into a stressed-out state of mind. Rather, be kind to yourself as you think your way from stressed-out to peaceful.

~

QUESTIONS TO THINK ABOUT

1. Do you live in a state of chronic stress?

2. What are the primary stressors in your life?

3. How would you describe your reactions to the stressors in your life?

4. What happens to you when you describe yourself as "stressed-out"?

5. Do you have a story to tell about someone like the young man at the San Francisco fireworks?

6. Do you have a story to tell about yourself when you were the one who got stressed-out by some unwanted experience?

7. How you do think about the stressors in your life?

8. How can you react peacefully to stressors in your life?

Chapter 2

Thinking About Stress

The greatest weapon against stress is our ability to choose one thought over another.

William James

What Is Stress?

The word *stress* comes from the Latin *strictus.* Consider these definitions from *Merriam-Webster:*

- Stress means to draw tight.
- Stress is a force exerted on a body that strains it or deforms its shape.
- Stress is also the resistance or cohesiveness of a body resisting such force.

The basic meaning of *strictus* is to *squeeze.* Think of a boa constrictor. Its name reveals its method of killing. It wraps its body around its prey and then slowly squeezes, squeezes, squeezes the life out of its victim. You experience this kind of constricting pressure when your shoes pinch your feet, your tie feels like a noose around your neck, or your belt is so tight that you can barely breathe.

Strictness applies to inflexible rules, rigid demands, and harsh teachers. In the old days—back when I was in elementary school—

teachers were supposed to be strict to teach us to obey the rules and never, ever get out of line. They were harsh, severe, and unsmiling. Strict rules, strict supervision, and strict teachers, parents, and leaders produce constricted lives.

According to the dictionary definitions, *stress* can refer to the cause—the pressure that squeezes you—and it can also refer to the effect—what it feels like to be squeezed. Although the word *stress* can be used correctly to refer to both cause and effect, I intend to make clear distinctions between cause and effect. I refer to *the cause of stress as a stressor* and *the effect of the stressor as stress.* The revised dictionary definitions then become:

- A stressor is a force exerted on a body that strains it or deforms its shape.
- Stress is the resistance or cohesiveness of a body resisting such force.

STRESS AND SHAPE

Visualize a balloon on a string. The balloon exists in its natural shape. Now, imagine pushing that balloon through a hole that is smaller than the balloon but big enough to squeeze the balloon through it. The only way to get the balloon through the hole is to deform its shape. You can't get a square block of wood through a smaller round hole, but you can push a pliable balloon through a hole smaller than the balloon.

The significant fact is that the balloon doesn't squeeze itself through the hole. The stressor does that by distorting the balloon and pushing it through the hole. In this example, you're the stressor—the cause of stress to the balloon. The effect on the balloon is stress as it is distorted, squeezed, pushed, and pulled to get through the hole—unless it breaks from the pressure of being squeezed. This is the distinction between a stressor and stress. Stress doesn't just happen. *Stress is a reaction to the actions of a stressor.*

Stressors distort the shape of something. Under-inflated balloons are flexible enough to be distorted into other shapes—including balloon animals for children's birthday parties. Other objects—such as brick walls that collapse under too much pressure—aren't so flexible.

Flexible objects can adapt to some distortion, but when the force is too great, the stress is intolerable. The hose bursts, the balloon breaks, the wall crumbles. Anything can reach the point of too much pressure, too much strain, too much constriction, too much restriction. This includes the effect of too much pressure on you.

HOW DOES STRESS DEFORM YOU?

Stress deforms. Whatever type of stress you experience in your life, the defining characteristic of all stress experiences is that you're being squeezed in a way that deforms you. The next time you feel stressed, ask yourself: How are you being deformed? What is being pushed and squeezed? What part of you is being distorted by the effect of the stressor? Sometimes you're being pressured by some external stressor and sometimes you are your own stressor.

Think of this when you're trying to force yourself to do something that doesn't fit you. You probably wouldn't try to cram your feet into shoes that are three sizes too small, but you might try to pressure yourself to take on something that doesn't fit. It could be a job or a project that requires you to distort yourself in some way. When this happens, the stressor is not something or someone outside of you. When this happens, you're the cause of your own stress.

STRESS AND STRAIN

Stress also strains. *Strain* has dictionary definitions with a range of meanings and connotations that overlap with *stress*. Both stress and strain can be nouns or verbs. For our purposes, *strain is maximum stress*. Strain is the result of maximum effort to exert force or to resist force. Both can lead to injury. In simple terms, strain is when either the stressor or the stressed reaches a breaking point.

As inanimate objects, balloons don't strain themselves by trying to squeeze themselves through holes. Only living beings can strain themselves. Strain results when you attempt to do something that is beyond your capacities, such as trying to lift an object that is too heavy or resist an overpowering force.

YOUR WEAPON AGAINST STRESS

The level of stress you experience relates directly to your reaction to stressors. You can choose how you react, why you react, and even if you react:

Consider this statement by William James:

> The greatest weapon against stress[ors] is our ability to choose one thought over another.

I have changed *stress* to *stressors* in this quotation to maintain the distinction between *stressor as cause* and *stress as effect*. Stressors can't control your thoughts and they can't control your reactions.

According to this distinction, your ability to *choose one thought over another* is your greatest weapon against stressors.

The word that stands out in James's statement is *weapon*. It's an Old English word for instruments of fighting and defense. *Merriam Webster* provides these definitions of *weapon*:

- Something (such as a gun, knife, club, or bomb) that is used for fighting or attacking someone or for defending yourself when someone is attacking you.
- Something (such as a skill, idea, or tool) that is used to win a contest or achieve something.

Weapons are instruments of war. These two definitions describe two contexts. In the first, a weapon is an instrument of actual warfare—a gun, knife, club, or bomb—when the stakes are life or death. In the second, a weapon has a metaphorical meaning—a skill, idea, or tool—when the stakes are winning a non-lethal conflict.

Whether you're involved in an actual or metaphorical war, you're in a life or death battle. Stressors are directly related to the quality of your life and your health, including how long and how well you live. Stressors can and do kill. Medical doctors confirm that much sickness, disease, and many debilitating health conditions result from stress.

A stressed-out life robs you of your happiness, your joy, your health, your peace, your creativity, and your love. What do you get in return? You experience anxiety, fear, sickness, worry, and depression.

In James's language, your thoughts are weapons of war. Your thoughts can be weapons of war that you use against yourself. They can also be weapons of war that you use to defend yourself. Most significantly, your thoughts can end the war and declare peace.

Underneath it all, your words are your most powerful weapons against stress. The claim that words are more powerful than weapons of war is an ancient idea. The first known version of the idea was by Ahiqar, who lived in ancient Assyria during the seventh century BC: "The word is mightier than the sword."   Although other writers expressed similar ideas throughout history, the most quoted phrase was written by Edward Bulwer-Lytton in 1839:

The pen is mightier than the sword.[2]

If your greatest weapon against stressors is your ability to choose one thought over another, your thoughts are the direct result of the words you use. If you change your words, you'll change your thoughts, and if you change your thoughts, you'll have powerful weapons to defeat the effect of stressors in your life.

It's easier to control what you say than what you feel. However, what you feel is directly related to what you say. If you react emotionally to a stressor, you can tone down your emotional response by the way you speak to yourself and to others. You don't have to be slave to your emotions if you change your thoughts.

WORDS TO CREATE A PEACEFUL LIFE

If your purpose is to transform a stressed-out life into a peaceful one, the world's most powerful tool is available for you to use, free of charge. In his best-selling book, *The Seven Habits of Highly Successful People,* Stephen R. Covey identifies the seventh habit as "sharpening the saw"—the habit of "continuous improvement."[3]

Just as hammers and saws are tools for carpenters, words are tools for creating the life you choose. All tools work best when you know how to use them and how to take care of them. Words are powerful tools that do best when you sharpen them and use them precisely. You can "sharpen the saw" with your language about stress and stressors.

Your primary goal is not to remove all potential stressors from your life—as if you could—but to see that what you're calling stress is something you created in response to stressors. If you created it, you can disarm it with more powerful weapons.

You begin by learning how to use your weapons effectively. You can start by paying close attention to the habitual language you use to describe stressors and their effects on you. If you continually respond to stressors with words about how "stressed-out" you are, you might as well be waving a white flag of surrender. The stressors have overpowered your defenses. However, you can use your words as your most powerful weapon of defense. You can begin by replacing "stressed-out" with more empowering words.

You rob yourself of your own power by seeing yourself—and using language describing yourself—as the hapless victim of something called "stress." By making clear in your own mind and in your own thoughts and in your own vocabulary that you recognize the difference between stressors and your reaction to those stressors, you claim the power of words and thoughts to turn stressed-out into peaceful.

~

QUESTIONS TO THINK ABOUT

1. How does stress deform you?

2. Consider specific stressors in your life. How do you feel strained and deformed by the stressors in your life?

3. How does your resistance to stressors create stress in your life?

4. What thoughts can you choose that would change the way you react to the stressors in your life?

5. What better description of yourself can you choose than "stressed-out"?

Chapter 3

Thinking About
Stress and Thought

The components of anxiety, stress, fear, and anger
do not exist independently of you in the world. They
simply do not exist in the physical world, even
though we talk about them as if they do.

Wayne Dyer

STRESS AND THOUGHT

The most powerful ability you have in your life is your capacity to
think. You can transform stressed-out into peaceful by thinking
about your own role in creating stress in your life. Consider Wayne
Dyer's claim that stress has no independent existence outside of you
by thinking about something that you consider stressful in your life.

How about *the holidays?* In the United States, "the holidays" have
become an annual stressed-out season for multitudes of women.
Many women feel stressed-out because of all that they *have to do.*
Buying gifts. Wrapping gifts. Preparing elaborate holiday meals.
Hosting parties. Attending parties. Traveling to visit families or
having families come to visit. The to-do list is long. Sometime in
November, these stressed-out women start asking each other the
inevitable question: "Are you ready for the holidays?" The answer is

usually no, followed by, "I can't wait for January second so it will all be over."

Stop and think carefully about this. If you're feeling stressed-out by the prospect of the holiday season, who or what is causing you to feel that way? If you think about it, you'll recognize that becoming stressed-out by the holidays has become a socially accepted condition that afflicts many women. (Men seem to be immune from the condition.) When you think about it, you'll very likely realize that much of this annual holiday stress is self-inflicted. Is anyone *forcing* you do any of this? Or, are you inflicting this stress upon yourself?

WHAT WOULD YOU CHANGE?

How would the thought that you're creating your own stress change how you think about the holiday season? If you're willing to challenge the idea that stress is as essential as Thanksgiving turkey, you can choose to be peaceful. You don't *have to* think that holiday stress is inevitable. You can even consider the radical thought that you can enjoy yourself in the holiday season without stressing out.

If you're willing to consider the possibility that your thoughts are creating your stressed-out feelings, what could you do to turn stress thoughts into peaceful thoughts? For example, what if your family tradition "requires" you to bake ten types of Christmas cookies? What thoughts could change "I have to bake ten types of Christmas cookies and I don't know when I am going to have the time" into a statement that isn't so oppressively stress-inducing?

You can think about it. Is there any part of baking Christmas cookies that you enjoy? Why do you *have to* bake *ten* kinds of cookies? Would *two* kinds of cookies be enough? Do you *have to* bake any cookies? If your thoughts cause you to feel stressed-out, what thoughts would turn stressed-out into peaceful? What thoughts would turn *have to* into *love to*? What thoughts could turn an annual stressed-out season into a season you enjoy?

THINKING ABOUT THINKING

Baking Christmas cookies might not be a stressful problem for you. What is? What *have-to-do-it* thoughts create stress in your life? How can you identify your stress-inducing thoughts and replace them with peace-creating thoughts? How can you change how you think about stress in your life?

For a fascinating guide to *thinking about thinking,* mull over these words by Albert Einstein in *How to Think Like Einstein,* by Scott Thorpe:

> It's not that I'm smart, it's just that I stay with the problems longer.[4]

Einstein was being a bit modest here, but Einstein made such breakthroughs in science precisely because he was willing to think deeply about problems. Rather than accept conventional wisdom, he started from a different place. He was known to think about problems longer than most people, which is why he challenged the dominant assumptions of physics.

One of Einstein's best known statements concerns the need to break the rules:

> There is nothing that is a more certain sign of insanity than to do the same thing over and over and expect the results to be different .[5]

If you want to change your stress-inducing thoughts, break the rules. Challenge the assumptions you take for granted. Be willing to think—really think—about your life and how you live it. Identify the assumptions you make. Think about how you derail yourself with your thoughts. Think about the difference between thoughts that create stress in your life and thoughts that create peace. You have enormous power to change your circumstances by thinking carefully about what you say and how your words affect you.

ASSUMPTIONS

One of my favorite quotations is this provocative statement about philosophical assumptions by the brilliant mathematician and philosopher Alfred North Whitehead:

> When you are criticizing the philosophy of an epoch, do not chiefly direct your attention to those intellectual positions which its exponents feel it necessary explicitly to defend. There will be some fundamental assumptions which adherents to all the variant systems within the epoch unconsciously presuppose. Such assumptions appear so obvious that people do not know what they are assuming because no other way of putting things has ever occurred to them. With these assumptions a certain limited number of types of philosophic systems are possible, and this group of systems constitutes the philosophy of the epoch.

Whitehead also said:

> I have suffered a great deal from writers who have quoted this or that sentence of mine either out of its context or in juxtaposition to some incongruous matter which quite distorted my meaning, or destroyed it altogether.

I respectfully cite Whitehead's quotation about philosophy—not because of what he claimed about philosophy—but because of what he claimed about *assumptions*. If we change the focus from *philosophy* to *stress*, these words identify what seems to be a fundamental assumption of our era—the assumption that "stressed-out" is an inevitable fact of life. This is the core assumption I'm challenging in this book. Consider the implications of Whitehead's words as they relate to assumptions about stress:

> There will be some fundamental assumptions [about stress] which adherents to all the variant [beliefs about stress] within the epoch unconsciously presuppose. Such assumptions [about stress] appear so obvious that people do not know what they are assuming [about stress] because no other way of putting things [about stress] has ever occurred to them.

TYPES OF STRESS EXPERIENCES

Once again, at the risk of doing exactly what Whitehead lamented, I again edit his words to make my own claim about simplistic statements about stress:

> [Stressed-out people] have suffered a great deal from writers who have [oversimplified the role of stressors] either out of context or in juxtaposition to some incongruous matter which quite [ignored their life experiences] or [denied them] altogether.

Simplistic claims about stress fail to differentiate between traumatic stress and chronic stress. They also fail to differentiate between the people who experience stress. Are you an able-bodied, intellectually competent, and financially capable adult who lives in a reasonably civilized part of the world? Or, are you a child, disabled, or financially dependent? Do you live in a dangerous and abusive family situation, a war zone, or a region of endemic poverty, rampant disease, or violence? Are you facing some potential catastrophe, such as an earthquake, wildfire, flood, blizzard, or hurricane? These distinctions matter.

PAYING ATTENTION TO YOUR THOUGHTS

What do you notice when you think about your language about stress, anxiety, fear, and anger? Do you talk about these emotions as forces that exist independently of you? Do you blame someone or something else for "making" you feel the way you do?

You can ask some questions about why and how you feel what you do:

- How do my thoughts cause me to feel stressed-out?

- How do my thoughts cause me to feel anxious, afraid, or angry?

- How do my thoughts persuade me that someone or something causes me to feel stressed-out?

When you think about your thoughts, you'll very likely realize that you're tearing yourself down, scaring yourself, worrying yourself, and upsetting yourself with your words and your thoughts rather than empowering yourself in your particular situation.

REAL OR IMAGINED POSSIBILITIES

The question to keep asking yourself concerns the difference between current reality and imagined possibilities:

- How much of my stress concerns current realities?

- How much of my stress concerns possibilities that I imagine might happen?

Life is filled with experiences that are unwanted, painful, expensive, and heartbreaking. Even in the worst circumstances, you can think about the connections between your thoughts, your words, and your stressed-out feelings. This awareness can transform your fears of imagined possibilities into self-trust about your ability to deal with what comes your way.

FEAR OF FEAR ITSELF

Consider these famous words from the first inauguration of Franklin D. Roosevelt as the 32nd President of the United States on March 4, 1933 in the midst of the Great Depression:

> So, first of all, let me assert my firm belief that the only thing we have to fear is fear itself—nameless, unreasoning, unjustified terror which paralyzes needed efforts to convert retreat into advance. In every dark hour of our national life a leadership of frankness and of vigor has met with that understanding and support of the people themselves which is essential to victory. And I am convinced that you will again give that support to leadership in these critical days.[6]

"The only thing we have to fear is fear itself." Roosevelt was talking about manufactured fear. The kind of fear that gets made up when you worry too much about what might happen. Made-up fears are like shadowboxing. You're fighting against an idea, an image, a possibility conjured up from imagining the worst.

You can set yourself free from this kind of obsessive worrying by calmly identifying the difference between a real threat and an imagined one, between real situation in the world and the imagined situation in your mind. A news alert that a tornado is heading your way is a legitimate cause for feeling stressed without becoming stressed-out. You don't ignore such warnings and you prepare for the worst. However, worrying about "what might happen sometime" is insufficient reason to stress out. When you let your thoughts run away with you, you're stressing yourself and making yourself feel helpless.

You can change those imaginations by changing your thinking. You can then focus on the real threats in the world, the real circumstances when you need to do something to deal with real dangers. Otherwise, you're frittering away your courage and your capacity in what Max Ehrmann called "dark imaginings" in his poem "Desiderata":

> Nurture strength of spirit to shield you in sudden misfortune.
>
> But do not distress yourself with dark imaginings.[7]

HOW TO CONTROL YOUR THOUGHTS

No one can control your thoughts except you. You can control what you say and what you think by being aware of what you're thinking. Do your thoughts empower you or do your thoughts keep you worried, fearful, upset, angry, and stressed-out?

What can you say to yourself about how to change your vocabulary? Ask yourself: Am I creating a mountain out of a molehill? Do my thoughts cause me to feel afraid? Am I creating my own fear by worry about what might happen? If you find yourself thinking thoughts that keep you fearful or stressed-out, try saying out loud: "Cancel that thought." Cancel that thought and substitute another thought. Treat it as a game rather than another *have to* in your life. Listen to your own language. Pay attention to what other people say. If you listen you'll often hear the same kind of self-induced stress in what other people say. You can't change their thoughts and words but you can decide to change yours.

THE POWER OF DECISION MAKING

What is a decision? The word means to *cut.* You can see the same root in the word *incision.* To *decide* is to *cut between choices.* Consider the sword as a symbol of decision making. You cut out all of the other choices in favor of one.

Decisions can be difficult. You go back and forth thinking about choices until you choose one rather than any other option. This is what thought does. You can also decide about stress. You can choose to keep the definition that stress happens to you or you can decide to live by the definition that you create stress with your thoughts.

~

QUESTIONS TO THINK ABOUT

1. What is your role in creating stress in your life?

2. Do you think that being stressed-out is an inevitable fact of life?

3. Do you have a history of traumatic stress?

4. Do your assumptions create chronic stress in your life?

5. How do your thoughts cause you to feel stressed-out, anxious, afraid, or angry?

6. How much of your stress concerns current realities?

7. How much of your stress concerns possibilities that you imagine might happen?

8. How can you change your reactions to stressors in your life by changing your words?

PART II

THINKING ABOUT
WHAT YOU SAY ABOUT STRESS

Chapter 4

Thinking About
Stress and Speech

No person is your friend who demands your
silence, or denies your right to grow.

Alice Walker

STRESS AND SUPPRESSION OF SPEECH

Silencing speech is one of the strongest causes of stress. Speaking
ability is one of the defining characteristics of humanity. Freedom of
speech is a fundamental tenet of human rights in the United States
Constitution. The First Amendment protects these rights:

> Congress shall make no law respecting an establishment of
> religion, or prohibiting the free exercise thereof; or
> abridging the freedom of speech, or of the press; or the
> right of the people peaceably to assemble, and to petition
> the Government for a redress of grievances.[8]

Despite this legal freedom to speak without being silenced by the
government, no laws exist to prevent people from being silenced by
the people in their lives. Many people know what it's like to be afraid
to speak. Freedom of speech is the first right taken away by tyrants,
bullies, and abusers. Throughout human history, the powerful have

silenced those they oppress. The demand for silence conceals oppression and abuse. Those who control your speech control you.

Suppression of speech is a powerful stressor. The freedom to say out loud what you're thinking and feeling is a deep urge within most people. How do you talk about your feelings and your desires? Do you dare to speak about your dreams? Or are your dreams ridiculed or criticized? Would anyone listen to you if you talked about what matters to you? How much does it cost you in suppressed energy to keep silent about what you really care about?

Stress is your constricting reaction to someone or something you perceive as potentially harmful to you. Are you too afraid to say something in response to what someone else has said or done? Are you free to object, to complain, to talk back? Or are you scared into silence? The more imbalance in power between the one who has freedom to say anything to you while you have no freedom to speak, the greater the stress you experience.

The one with power speaks. The one without power is forbidden to speak. To be silenced is to experience powerful stressors that take the form of threats of what will happen to you if you speak. Whether the threat is overt—"I will kill you if you tell"—or whether it's implicit, if you're the one who is silenced you know that your survival depends on remaining silent and keeping secrets.

Being forced to comply with such demands is a powerful stressor. You're being commanded to do something against your will because you'll lose something if you don't. How do you respond to such threats? Do you speak despite the threats? Do you submit to enforced silence? Do you tell anyone else? Whatever you do, threats that demand your silence are profoundly stressful and can have lifelong consequences.

SILENCED WITH A THREAT

This topic has particular relevance for me. One of the dominating occurrences of my own hellish childhood was to hear the bellowing voice demanding silence. In addition to daily demands for silence, I endured the occasional mega-stress-inducing experience of one of our family car trips from hell.

In those ordeals, my three brothers and I were ordered to ride in the car in complete silence as we bounced along pre-interstate bumpy and winding roads for four hundred and forty miles to visit grandparents in another state. We sat in obedient silence for mile after mile with no one talking to anyone, including the bully behind the wheel who drove in sullen silence. The radio was off to prevent "running down the battery." Meanwhile, the non-stop cigarette smoke filled the car with more and more noxious fumes. Windows had to remain closed because open windows would give the driver "a stiff neck." The toxic air resulted in several emergency stops for either my youngest brother or me to throw up by the side of the road. Such inconvenience to the driver triggered a stream of obscenities and profanities.

Throwing up meant trading places with my brother until we were both drained. The last one to throw up rode in the front seat. I always hoped I would the last one to throw up so I could spend the rest of the trip in the front seat, rather than in the middle of the back seat. In the back seat, I sat with my feet on the hump in the floor of the Buick. My older brothers silently tormented me by pushing their legs against mine. I sat squeezed in the middle with my feet up on the hump and my legs compressed. It was all done silently of course. No one was allowed to speak and I was not allowed to complain.[9]

PAINFULLY SHY

Meanwhile, my daily life consisted of ongoing abuse accompanied by the demand that I must never, ever say anything about what happened at home. I never did, not until I was old enough to get out of that place, away from harm's way. I was too frightened by the threats of being killed if I ever told anyone anything. You won't be surprised to know that I was a painfully shy and silent child.

The description of being "painfully shy" is appropriate. Anyone who is described as painfully shy is in pain. If you look, you can see the pain in the eyes of abused children. You can see the pain in the women—and men—who endure marriage to batterers. You can see it in the eyes of anyone who endures suffering because of racism or sexism or ageism. Anytime you see abuse inflicted on the powerless, you'll see pain lying beneath the silence if you look.

Those who "suffer in silence" are everywhere. Demands for silence to cover abuse are powerful stressors. If you have your own story to tell about being scared into silence, you know all too well what it feels like.

CHOOSE CAREFULLY WHAT YOU DO AND WHAT YOU SAY

What about your experience of stress when the stressor is not explicitly life-threatening? Have you ever tried to have a conversation with someone when you're monitoring every word you say to prevent an outburst? When you're walking on eggshells not to offend someone who is easily offended? When you don't want to trigger an explosion of rage? If you have, you know how it feels to silence yourself out of fear that you'll say the wrong thing.

Powerful stressors constrain the inhabitants of the wizard world in the *Harry Potter* stories when they're afraid to say out loud the name of Voldemort—"he who must not be named." Powerful stressors constrain families at family gatherings when everyone is afraid to talk about the one topic that is primary in everyone's mind— "the elephant in the living room." Powerful stressors constrain you any time you have to be careful about what you say, how you say it, and when you say it.

SILENCING YOURSELF ABOUT YOURSELF

How do you communicate about your life? Or do you? What secrets do you keep? Do you tell the truth or do you suppress it? Do you hide what you're feeling behind a veneer of laughter? Some people go through life keeping their distance. They might as well be wearing "Go Away" signs around their necks. Other people hide behind sociable masks.

One way to cover pain is to tell jokes. The late Robin Williams demonstrated the power of hidden hurt. People who knew him best talked about the sadness that came over him when he was off stage, off screen. How many times have you heard about someone committing suicide and then heard the people who "knew" the suicide say they had no idea anything was wrong. You often don't know from the outside what untold secrets people are carrying.

Do you suppress talking about your beliefs? Beliefs inhabit especially tricky terrain. Conventional wisdom warns against discussing religion and politics. Linus in *It's the Great Pumpkin, Charlie Brown* puts it this way:

> There are three things I have learned never to discuss with people...religion, politics, and the Great Pumpkin.[10]

What happens when you're in the presence of people who have different beliefs and attempt to convince you? When do you argue back? When do you suppress your opinions? Whatever you do, talking about and not talking about religion and politics can be mighty stressors.

TALKING ABOUT OTHERS

Do you ever tell someone that you're "dying to talk" about something? Such figures of speech often reveal lived reality. If you're "dying to talk," the words say that you'll die if you don't say it. Maybe it's just an empty expression. Or maybe, the words tell you something important about what you're keeping unsaid within you. What within you would die if you don't say what you feel compelled to say? Suppression of speech—whether you do it by monitoring your speech or whether you're being bullied into silence—produces self-protecting, self-induced stress. Even if the stress doesn't kill your body, it can kill your spirit, your happiness, and your dreams.

How much of your speech involves saying out loud what you would really like to say to someone, but you don't. Instead, you find a substitute. The substitute can be a friend who is willing to listen to you complain about why you can't talk to the person who is "driving you crazy." These words describe a stressor—the words or actions someone is doing or saying, or not doing or saying—that result in stress in you.

Notice what you're saying about yourself with the language of *driving you crazy:* You say that you're being driven somewhere by someone else. As a metaphor, it proclaims that you feel powerless because someone else has control of the steering wheel. How often does this metaphor reveal your perception that you're powerless in an unwanted situation?

Ponder once again the claim that feeling stressed-out is your self-created reaction to a stressor. The outrageous, cruel, mean, unfair, or otherwise unwanted words and actions of someone else are external stressors. "Going crazy" is your reaction. A provocative question for you to ponder is:

> Are you really being driven crazy by someone else or are you the one who is doing the driving?

GOSSIP

Gossip is *talking about* other people. Gossip can take many forms. One directly related to your perceptions of power or powerlessness concerns telling friends what you'd really like to say to someone else. This kind of gossip is another kind of speech suppression. If you'd like to tell off someone, why don't you do it? What would be the cost of telling off your boss? Or your mother? Or your father? Or anyone else you don't dare to tell off?

Every kind of social structure has its own pecking order. The social hierarchy of the barnyard—from the roosters to the hens to the chicks—allows those with more power to peck the less powerful. The most powerful do the pecking. The powerless get pecked.

Gossip is a way demonstrating how the pecking order works for people. The most powerful people can say just about anything with no consequences. What they say about other people is never called gossip. The ones on the bottom learn early that talking back can get them in big trouble. Perhaps that's why women are more often characterized as gossips than men. Girls and women learn early to be deferential to male authority and power. They also learn that it's safer to *talk about* more powerful people rather than confront them. They vent their frustrations by means of gossip.

Much of the complaining that people do day after day is saying out loud what they don't dare say to the people who are more powerful. Speaking out of turn or telling off the wrong person can have consequences. Gossip allows you to vent frustrations, but it doesn't address the real problem: You feel powerless about a stressor. This leads to another question for you to mull over:

> Does gossip relieve your stress or do you create stress by gossiping?

CONSEQUENCES

What are the consequences of not telling the truth as you see it? In the old *Archie Bunker* TV show, Archie was repeatedly telling Edith to *stifle* herself. The primary meaning of the verb stifle is to "choke, suffocate, drown." To stifle is to deprive of air so that you can't breathe. When you learn to stifle yourself because it's too dangerous to speak, the stifling leads to a slow death of will, of spirit, of joy, of happiness, of creativity. Stifling leads to resignation and obedience to power. A stifled life becomes a joyless exercise in going through the motions doing what you're told to do. It's the horse that had its spirit broken. The dog that was abused too often. The child who learned to be afraid.

The ones who are stifled by abuse, oppression, and restrictive social and religious rules slowly suffocate in mind and spirit long before they take their last breath. Abuse and oppression come in many forms, but one of the first that goes is real freedom of speech. Dreams die when speech dies in people who say what they're told to say. Courage dies in yes-men and yes-women who don't dare disagree with the powerful. Enthusiasm dies in terrified children who do not dare to tell the secrets. Dreams and hopes and aspirations die when speech is forbidden. Stifling leads to stressed-out suffering in silence.

~

QUESTIONS TO THINK ABOUT

1. Do you have freedom to speak or is your freedom to speak suppressed?

2. Who or what suppresses your speech?

3. How does suppression of your speech create stress in your life?

4. Are you painfully shy? Why?

5. When do you have to choose carefully what you say?

6. Do you keep secrets about your life?

7. How does gossip relate to suppression of your speech?

8. Do you stifle yourself because you're afraid to speak?

Chapter 5

Thinking About Stress and Vision

The only thing worse than being blind is having sight but no vision.

Helen Keller

STRESS AND VISION

Stress robs you of vision. Vision is not equivalent to sight. Sight refers to the function of your eyes. Vision refers to your capacity to imagine what you can't see. These distinctions mean that you can have perfect eyesight and lack vision, or you can be blind and have transformative vision. This distinction is why Helen Keller, who was both blind and deaf, couldn't see but had vision beyond the present, and why others with 20/20 eyesight can't imagine beyond their current circumstances.[12]

Imagine means seeing an image in your mind. Visionaries imagine possibilities beyond anything that exists. Visionaries have ranged from mystics to inventors, dreamers to doers. Martin Luther King was one of the great visionaries of his era—of any era. He envisioned a world beyond racial division.

What's your vision of your future? Can you see it? Does it feel possible or just a pipe dream? Do you imagine yourself accomplishing what you see? Or are you just wishing and hoping your life will be better?

Stress constricts your vision. When you feel stressed-out, you feel squeezed into a tight space with no way out. Your life becomes a close-up in a picture where most of the image has been cropped to magnify one small section of the whole picture. All you can see is a small fragment of the whole. Stress tells you that this fragment is the whole. This is the way it is. The way it will always be. You're helpless with no hope for a better future. If you can see only what's current in your life, how can you envision a peaceful future?

YOUR PLASTIC BRAIN

Your greatest asset to imagine a different future is your *plastic* brain. This doesn't mean that you have the "brain" of the Marvel Super Heroes, such as the Hulk, Captain America, and Thor, or of Barbie, Dora the Explorer, or one of the *Frozen* sisters, Anna or Elsa.

The word *plastic* originated from Latin *plasticus*, from Greek *plastikos*, which means "molded." The original connotation of the word "plastic" defined solid substances that can be molded. Since then, the word plastic has taken on additional meanings and can also refer to any material that undergoes a permanent change of shape. The plastic (brainless) heads of the Hulk or Barbie can't change. However, your plastic brain never stops changing.

This *plasticity* enables your brain to change physically, functionally, and chemically throughout your life:

Brain plasticity—also called neuroplasticity—is an odd term for most people, with the word "plastic" causing images of Tupperware or Saran Wrap to pop into your head. However, brain plasticity is a common term used by neuroscientists, referring to the brain's ability to change at any age—for better or worse. As you would imagine, this flexibility plays an incredibly important role in our brain development (or decline) and in shaping our distinct personalities.[13]

Your brain's capacity to change offers hopeful possibilities for stressed-out brains. Whether your stress is recent, the product of early life stress, or the result of a traumatic experience, your plastic brain *can* change for the better.

CHRONIC STRESS AND YOUR BRAIN

Stress affects your brain and also produces copious amounts of cortisol. Cortisol is a steroid hormone produced by the adrenal cortex in response to stressors. When you're in a state of stress, your higher mind—the various components of the cerebrum—doesn't work very well. However, your emergency danger system is fully operational. It keeps you edgy, hyper-alert, hyper-aware of potential threats. Unable to relax. Unable to sleep. Unable to let your guard down. Stressed-out feelings and thoughts overpower your ability to think clearly and to imagine beyond your current circumstances. The liberating truth is that you can become a visionary of your own life by changing your brain.

POST-TRAUMATIC STRESS

It's important to acknowledge the difference between a current stressful situation and chronic stress. Chronic stress and high levels of cortisol in early life change both brain function and structure. Post-traumatic stress disorder (PTSD) also changes brain function and structure. Both *hurt* and *trauma* can refer to physical, mental, and emotional pain and injury:

- *Hurt* refers to pain or injury.
- *Trauma* refers to more serious pain or injury.

Hurts can be painful and cause great suffering and inconvenience but hurts can heal without affecting your identity and without creating profound brain-changing stress. Hurts don't have the same power to bind you to your painful event as traumas. This distinction is why medicine refers to *post-traumatic stress disorder* (PTSD). It doesn't have a diagnosis named *post-hurt stress disorder*. Traumas produce powerful stressors that deeply affect your identity and your brain.

PTSD can result from one horrific experience. It can also result from ongoing exposure to stressors over a long period of time. This description of the development of PTSD in police officers is particularly insightful:

> A sense of impending doom combined with helplessness to avert it (the hallmarks of trauma) can build up over time, with repeated exposure to stressful and violent events.[14]

In addition to police, vulnerable candidates for PTSD range across a broad spectrum from military personnel in combat zones to children who live in stressful and violent families. The combination of helplessness and fear for your life becomes a powerful legacy that can endure for a lifetime without help.

It's far beyond the scope of this book and my qualifications to describe the effects of chronic and traumatic stress on the structure and function of the brain. However, knowing that your brain is plastic provides encouraging news for anyone who experienced brain-changing stress, including PTSD. Since your brain has the capacity to change throughout your life, it's never too late for you to learn how to change your brain by changing the way you think.

LANGUAGE TO REMOLD YOUR BRAIN

A powerful source of stressors in your life is language itself. You can actually remold your brain by changing your language. Your language is one aspect in your life that is under your control. You can change your brain by becoming the editor of your own speech. You can even make a game out of it by playing your own version of a "drinking game" (without the drinks). The game is to keep track of how many times you say or think some word or phrase.

CAN'T OR COULD

You could begin by revising your language about helplessness. A telltale clue is the word *can't*. How many times do you say that you *can't* do something? When you say that you *can't*, you're expressing your belief that you have no other options. If you keep telling yourself that you *can't* do it, you've made *can't* your reality. You really can't do it. You're stuck. *Can't* is the language of no options. In contrast, *could* is the language of possibilities. *Could* expands your vision of what's possible. Whatever else is happening in your life, you can pay attention to your words and ask yourself whether you're using words of helplessness or possibility.

SHOULD

Another revealing word is *should*. Pay attention to how many times you see it in what you read, how often you hear it in what other people say, how often you say it, how often you tell yourself what you *should* do, or *should not* do. You might be astonished at the pervasiveness of this word in common language.

We're immersed in a sea of *shoulds*. When you start listening for it, and watching for it, you'll discover that *should* is one of the most common words in daily use in the English language. Then stop and think about what this means. *Should* is a command or advice to do or not do something. If you aren't doing it, you *should*. If you are doing it, you *shouldn't*. Then contemplate how the words *should* or *shouldn't* affect what you do or don't do and how you feel about your life. How would your life change if you replaced *should* with *could*? *Could* is a word about possibilities rather than a judgment about what you're doing or not doing.

HAVE TO OR CHOOSE TO

The word *could* leads to the language of *choice*. You can *choose* to pay attention your language and your thoughts. Do your words and thoughts describe you as someone who makes choices or as someone who has no choices? When you add choice to your daily vocabulary, you not only define your goals and aspirations, you're also imagining possibilities for your present and your future.

You can try this word experiment. The next time you hear yourself saying, "I have to," substitute the verb. Change your thought or say out loud "I choose to." Pick something mundane. Instead of saying "I have to do the laundry now," substitute "I choose to do the laundry now." Doing the laundry changes from *have-to* into *choose-to*.

If you think about it, every time you say "I have to do the laundry" and you go and do it, you're making the choice to do the laundry. You could also say "I have to do the laundry but I'm not going to do it." If you do the laundry without someone forcing you to do it, you're already making a choice. If you match your language to your actions, you're reinforcing the idea that you already have choices about how you live your life.

THE LAW OF UNDULATION

An insightful metaphor about life changes—including changes in your brain—is the "law of undulation" by C. S. Lewis in his book, *The Screwtape Letters. Undulation* is an up and down movement. The story is from the perspectives of the demons in hell who want to turn a Christian believer into a non-believer. The theological foundation of the metaphor is irrelevant to wisdom of the metaphor. The demon says that all humans believe that where they are right now is where they'll always be. When they're up, they believe they'll always be up. When they're down, they believe they'll always be down.[15]

Lewis's law of undulation won't be added to Newton's laws of motion in physics textbooks, but the idea itself is worth pondering. We humans have a tendency to believe that our current circumstances are defined by something like Newton's First Law of Motion:

> When viewed in an inertial reference frame, an object either remains at rest or continues to move at a constant velocity, unless acted upon by an external force.[16]

We tend to believe that our current circumstances are permanent. The way things are now are the way things will always be. The law of undulation is a reminder that life is never static. Whatever your current situation now, it will change.

LIFE ON A FERRIS WHEEL

The Navy Pier Ferris Wheel in Chicago demonstrates the law of undulation. From a distance, the wheel appears motionless. When you get closer, you realize that it's moving in continuous slow motion. Unlike typical carnival Ferris wheels, the wheel doesn't stop to allow riders to get on or off. Instead, you get on and off a continually moving wheel. Life on Earth shares this characteristic with the Navy Pier Ferris Wheel. Earth doesn't stop moving to let you on or off. Ups and downs are inevitable. Your life will change over time, no matter what you do or don't do.

Metaphors work best if you don't push them too far. You don't have to make the Ferris wheel a metaphor that rules your life. You can add additional metaphors. An obvious one is that you can drive a car. When you get behind the wheel, you're the one controlling the car. Whether it stops or starts, where it goes, how fast it goes, whether you take the next exit or stay on the same route, you're the one making the decisions.

Compare the difference between the verbs. You *ride* on a Ferris wheel. You *drive* a car. You're *told* when to get on and get off the

Ferris wheel. You *decide* when to get on the road and when to get off it when you drive. You *cannot change* the direction of the Ferris wheel goes. You *can change* the direction when you drive.

Once again, it's best not to push any metaphor too far. Why do you go for a ride on a Ferris wheel? You do it because it's fun. You even pay for the experience. You know that you're the passive rider who has no control over the Ferris wheel. You know that you'll go up and down. You also know that when the ride is over, you'll get off.

THE INEVITABILITY OF CHANGE

The universe we inhabit exists in a state of constant movement and constant change. Galaxies move as they are born and die in dramatic bursts of energy. Our Sun moves. Earth moves. Atoms move. Continents move. Oceans open and close. For galaxies and suns and planets, for continents and oceans and mountains, time is measured in millions—even billions—of years. The Atlantic Ocean grows two inches wider each year. The Himalayas grow higher and the Appalachians shrink year by year, but we humans, with our short lifespans don't notice because our sense of time is so short. However, nature around us changes, ever so slowly or in dramatic spurts of power. Earth exists in a state of deep time. Earth experiences tiny, tiny changes over eons as well as sudden unexpected changes. Volcanoes erupt and change landscapes. Hurricanes knock down trees. Floods change the flow of rivers.

Meanwhile, each of us is undergoing constant change. You're living on a Ferris wheel named Earth and both your life and your brain are constantly changing. However, unlike a Ferris wheel that takes you around in a loop, the undulations in your life also move you forward in time.

A STORY OF CHANGE

The movie *Groundhog Day* is a story about a man stuck in a time loop. Phil Connors relives the same day over and over again—except that each day is never the same. Although Phil believes that nothing will ever change, that he's stuck permanently in a situation he cannot escape, he does change. Day after day, he does things differently. Over time, his actions change who he is. He evolves from being an unhappy, egoistical, cruel person to a person who does kind actions for others and loves without manipulation.

The insight of the story is that you can change over time. You don't have to allow the sameness of your circumstances to trap you into an endless time loop. You don't have to be stuck, even if you do live in the same place, and go to the same job, and drive the same car day after day. All of these externals will eventually change in some way or another, even as you change day-by-day. People in your life will come and go. You'll meet new people. Meanwhile, you're getting older day-by-day. Life change is inevitable. Whatever your current experience, you can imagine a better future by the changing the way you think.

~

QUESTIONS TO THINK ABOUT

1.   Do you feel hopeful about your future?

2.   Do you feel stuck with no way out?

3.   How does awareness of the plasticity of your brain change the way you think about present and past stress in your life?

4.   Are you willing to change your daily language about helplessness?

5.   How often do you say "I can't"?

6.   How often do you say "I should" or "I shouldn't"?

7.   How often do you say "I have to"?

8.   Are you willing to choose other words?

9.   Do you believe that you can change your life by your thoughts, words, and actions?

Chapter 6

Thinking About Stress and Perspective

> The significant problems we face cannot be solved at the same level of thinking we were at when we created them.
>
> Albert Einstein

STRESS AND PERSPECTIVE

If you feel overwhelmed by stress, it's time to change your perspective. Perspective is your point of view, your angle of vision, your frame of reference.

Albert Einstein said that you can't solve problems at the same level of thinking you were when you created them. No one can see the whole of anything from one vantage point. As long as you look at stress and stressors in your life from the same perspective, you'll find it difficult to change them. A different perspective will always open up some new level of thinking.

You can change your perspective when you choose to be *observant*. Observant is an adjective to describe one who is watching. The observer is not the doer. You are observant when you look dispassionately at your circumstances without getting involved. People who describe their near-death experiences frequently talk about detachment from their bodies as they look down on themselves lying in a hospital bed. Whatever the validity of such claims, you can gain a different perspective on a stressful experience by emotionally detaching yourself and observing your reactions to a stressor.

Consider the perspective of a hawk. It flies high overhead, looking for prey. A small animal on the ground has little chance of escaping the keen eyesight of the hawk. With the benefit of its high perspective, the hawk can swoop down upon the helpless prey. What would you see about stress in your life if you could look at your life with a hawk-like perspective?

BENEFITS OF PERSPECTIVE

Looking at a stressor from a different perspective allows you see beyond the moment. Without perspective, a current problem can become the defining problem of your existence. Molehills become mountains. Trivial details become huge obstacles. Small errors become enormous blunders.

Think of the photographs people take when they play with perspective. You might see a picture of someone holding up a finger and thumb with the Eiffel Tower within it. The picture distorts reality. You know it's a distortion when the Eiffel Tower can fit between a finger and a thumb. However, you might not recognize distortions in other perceptions. Since what you see can be accurate or it can distort reality, it's important to verify what you think you're seeing by changing your point of view rather than standing in the same spot and insisting that what you see is the whole truth.

If you're feeling stuck in some situation and you keep reviewing your circumstances in the same way, you'll be unable to see beyond your current vision. A change in perspective can also change your reaction to a stressor. As long as you keep looking from the same spot, you won't see anything differently. If you can't see anything other than outside forces that make your life miserable, change the angle. Get closer. Move away from it. Look from above. Look from below. When you're willing to change your perspective, you can see new possibilities.

OBSERVING STRESS

Being the observer of your own life empowers you to overcome potentially stressful experiences. You can start by being observant about the stressor. Is it really about you? Or is someone having a bad day and taking it out on you? Do you take something personally that is not about you at all? Can you do something about it? Is it worth getting upset about it?

What if someone treats you rudely or says something cruel? Just because someone says something about you doesn't make it true. If you get upset, you give power to an untrue assessment. On the other hand, what if what someone says about you is accurate? How do you respond to what is true even if harshly spoken?

These questions are not easy. However asking them can make your life easier and much less stressful. Whatever the situation, and however you choose to respond to it, you'll benefit by observing the situation from your hawk-like perspective. Gain some distance before you decide to do something you'll regret. Especially, gain some distance if you feel offended, angry, or hurt.

A detached view from more than one angle saves you from getting hung up in trivial details and missing the big picture. You're better able to contrast the large with the small, the important with the less important. Perspective enables you to see when you're majoring in minors, straining gnats and swallowing camels, and missing the forest for the trees.

THE PERSPECTIVE OF HOPE

A powerful resource to change your perspective is your capacity to hope. Consider these words by Dale Carnegie:

> Most of the important things in the world have been accomplished by people who have kept on trying when there seemed to be no hope at all.

In a world of constant change, no matter what you're enduring now, hope imagines a different future. Hope isn't wishful thinking. Rather, hope holds a vision of the best even in the worst of times. Hope is the belief that this too will pass. Hope focuses on more than this moment by knowing that the world does change. The Sun does rise and set. Earth does spin around in its orbit. Springs do follow winters. Change is inevitable.

The perspective of hope that makes the difference between feeling stressed-out or feeling peaceful is to know that this moment— no matter how bad it is—is not the full picture. This moment is not the way things always will be. In such moments, you can gain strength and comfort by remembering Desmond Tutu's words:

> Hope is being able to see that there is light despite all of the darkness.

Norman Cousins, author of *Anatomy of an Illness*, which recounted his personal triumph over severe illness, believed that human emotions—particularly hope—are essential to overcoming illness. He said this about hope:

> The capacity for hope is the most significant fact of life. It provides human beings with a sense of destination and the energy to get started.

Cousins received an honorary degree in medicine and became an adjunct professor in the School of Medicine at UCLA where he did research on the biochemistry of human emotions and illness.

After ten years on the medical faculty, he wrote *Head First: The Biology of Hope*, about the results of his research. These words summarize his belief about the effect of hope on human biology:

> People tell me not to offer hope unless I know hope to be real, but I don't have the power not to respond to an outstretched hand. I don't know enough to say that hope can't be real. I'm not sure anyone knows enough to deny hope. I have seen too many cases these past ten years when death predictions were delivered from high professional station only to be gloriously refuted by patients for reasons having less to do with tangible biology than with the human spirit, admittedly a vague term but one that may well be the greatest force of all within the human arsenal.[17]

HOPE OR PROMISE

Hope is not the same as promise. Promise is a relationship word. Someone else declares, "I promise that I will do this for you," or "I promise that this event will happen." In contrast, hope is internal. You can hope that other people fulfill their promises to you, but whether they do or not, hope is something you do for yourself.

Thought is your medium of hope. Your emotions are much more volatile and difficult to change than thoughts. Emotions are like clouds that float in the sky, wisps of vapor blowing in the wind. In contrast, you can change your thoughts by the way you think.

Thoughts allow you to separate your thinking about a stressor from your emotional reaction to the stressor. Thoughts allow you to measure the cost of getting angry and upset. Is it worth it? You can think thoughts of hope rather thoughts of despair. As you think, your emotions will follow your thoughts.

You can also think about what serenity and peacefulness would mean for you. You can think about what is upsetting your serenity. You can think about the person whose words or actions triggered your emotional reaction. And then you can think about whether or not this stressor is worth upsetting your peace of mind.

We come back to where we started. The most effective way to change your life is to observe the problems of your life from different perspectives. A perspective of hope reminds you that this moment will pass. Hope means more than wanting your life to be different. Hope is your belief in a better time. Your perspective of hope in the midst of whatever stressors you're now experiencing is a powerful creative force to change your life.

~

QUESTIONS TO THINK ABOUT

1. How can you change your perspective about stressors in your life?
2. Do you have hope for your future?
3. What do you think about Norman Cousins's claim that your capacity for hope is the most significant fact of your life?
4. How can you make thought your medium of hope?
5. What would serenity and peacefulness mean for you?

PART III

THINKING ABOUT STRESSORS AND TIME

Chapter 7

Thinking About Stress and Time

Yesterday's the past, tomorrow's the future, but today is a gift. That's why it's called the present.

Bil Keane

STRESS AND TIME

Of all the stressors in our contemporary world, one that afflicts many of us is the perception that *we don't have enough time* to do what we "have to do" and *we can't spare the time* to do what we "want to do." This is why thinking about stressors means thinking carefully about your relationship with time. How do your thoughts about time create stress in your life?

One characteristic of stress is impatience. Impatience tells you that you don't have enough time. Impatience is the White Rabbit in Lewis Carroll's book, *Alice in Wonderland,* rushing through life proclaiming: "Oh dear! Oh dear! I shall be too late." In Disney's animated version, the White Rabbit sings a little song:

I'm late! I'm late! For a very important date! No time to say hello, goodbye! I'm late! I'm late! I'm late![18]

Is this you? Do you go through life proclaiming, "I'm late, I'm late, I'm late" for just about everything you do? A dominant verb of the

"I'm late, I'm late, I'm late" perspective on life is that you have to *grab* things because you're running so fast to get things done. How many times have you seen this in advertising? Because you're so busy, busy, busy, you can grab and go, eat and run. Since you don't have time to cook a real meal, you can pop frozen dinners into the microwave.

Does your to-do list stretch from now to forever? Are you always behind schedule, behind quota, always late? Who set the time schedule? Did you? Did someone else tell you have you have to get it done? If you're can't manage to keep on time according to your own timetable of doing it faster, you're setting yourself up to feel that you're constantly failing. "I'm late, I'm late, I'm late" creates a daily experience of stress.

If you spend your life rushing and grabbing, always on the go, and always telling yourself that you're late, you're surrendering the quality of your life to an idea—a thought that rules your life—the idea that you don't have enough time.

BELIEFS ABOUT WASTING TIME

What are your beliefs about wasting time? Do you share the sentiment expressed in these words from the poem "If" by Rudyard Kipling?:

> If you can fill the unforgiving minute with sixty seconds worth of distance run...[19]

This is a tough demand. Even the idea of "distance run" conjures up the image of the runner who is running, running, running. A minute has only sixty seconds. If you have to run for sixty seconds each minute, you have no time for anything else.

Although "If" is a rousing poem, this relationship with time sets an impossible objective. It's a belief based on the idea that if you aren't "doing something productive," you're *wasting time*. A question worth asking is NOT whether you're running every moment of your life, but whether you're living—truly living—your life. Can you live your life well if you keep running, running, running, filling every minute with activity? Or do Kipling's words define a life that's poorly lived?

CLOCK TIME AND THE QUALITY OF YOUR LIFE

Kipling's words reinforce the connection between clock time and quality of life. He refers to "the unforgiving minute." While poetically powerful, this kind of all-encompassing assessment of how you use your time can be a particularly oppressive judgment on how you live. It adds guilt to your experience of stress. Guilt and stress are a potent mix that prevents you from taking a long look at your life by considering this question: Is this the kind of life you choose to live?

If you stop long enough to ponder your frantically busy life, you might realize that you're not happy with the life you're living. You might realize that you're not fulfilling your almost-forgotten dreams. Whatever your dreams are, whatever dreams you used to have, they probably don't involve images of you in an endless race to do things you don't want to do, in a job you don't want, to serve the purposes of something you don't think is all that important.

You might realize that you're spending the time of your life on activities that aren't worth the cost. Pay particular attention to the verb here. You *spend* time to pay the cost. *Spend* is also the language of money. You spend money to pay costs. Here, the currency is time rather than money. The difference between the two is that money is potentially limitless. However, your time is limited to twenty-four hours each day. Do you want to spend the time of your life doing what you truly don't care about?

Contrary to Kipling's criterion for living a successful life, life isn't a race or an endurance contest. Life is the experience of being alive. Life isn't meant to be a race in which you keep running and never stop. Living also includes time to "stop and smell the roses."

MULTITASKING

Nothing demonstrates a frantic, counterproductive relationship with time more than the idea of *multitasking*. Multitasking is when you attempt to do more than one thing at once. Multitasking is actually *multiswitching*. Computers can work this way, because they're so fast, but multiswitching in human beings wastes time because you need to switch your focus back and forth from one task or topic to another.

Getting something done well requires sustained focus. Focus concentrates your attention on what you're doing for enough time to get it done well. Gary Keller makes this insightful observation:

> You can do two things at once but you can't focus effectively on two things at once.

These words get to the essence of what's wrong with the whole idea of multitasking. You can do two things at once, but you won't do either one very well.

It's an illusion—a delusion—to think than you can "multitask" successfully. Surely you have attempted to have a telephone conversation with someone who's multitasking. While you're on the phone, you discover that the person on the other end of the line is also having an email conversation with someone else. It's also possible that the multitasking multiswitcher is also involved in some other form of electronic communication that you don't know about. As you wait during the long pauses in the conversation, you experience the frustration of trying to have a conversation with someone who isn't fully present. Contrary to the claims of those who would have you believe that they can multitask effectively, multitasking multiswitching wastes everyone's time.

Every time you take your focus off what you're doing to do something else, even for a few minutes, you waste time because changing focus takes time. This is when mistakes happen. You lose track of what you were doing and have to remind yourself when you start again. Interruptions lead to mistakes, oversights, and increased time to get something done.

TIME AND YOUR IDENTITY

The belief that you don't have enough time also defines your perspective about your identity. You declare to yourself and the world that you aren't capable of keeping up. All of this rushing around creates your identity as someone who's always on the go to someplace else but never getting there on time. Your actions define you as Indispensable and yet Unreliable.

You're also known as Impatient. You're impatient with yourself and with others. You're impatient with the idea that some things take time. You're not alone. The belief that there's never enough time drives a stressed-out population.

No one has more time than anyone else, but not everyone becomes frantic about "not enough time." Some extraordinarily successful people are actually quite relaxed about time. Since you can't get more time, what can you change about your relationship with time for you to live a more peaceful, successful, and happy life?

You can begin by asking yourself some tough questions:

- Why do you feel that you must accomplish so much in your twenty-four hour day?
- Has it become a badge of honor to be stressed-out?
- Are you proud of yourself because you're so busy?

Does "I'm so stressed-out" become a way to compare your life to others? If you listen to people talk with each other—especially women with young children—you'll see a kind of contest going on to see who wins the prize for being most stressed-out.

Being stressed-out can become an identity, a way to compare yourself to others. You're so important, so needed, so irreplaceable, because you have to do so much for others. You have to go here and there, fix lunches, go to work, shop and cook and clean, help with homework, take children to classes and games and play dates, and much, much more. All of this busyness is a way to be proud about how stressed-out you are. To take time out for yourself is a dereliction of duty. Everyone depends on you. The world will fall apart without you.

HOW MUCH DOES IT COST?

Actually, the world won't fall part without you. Life will go on whatever you do. The critical question isn't about how you can get more done but how much does your impatience cost you? If you feel stressed-out most of the time, your impatience is costing you too much. It's costing you the experience of living a full, peaceful, happy life.

If stress is your constant companion, it's a clear sign that you would benefit from a revised relationship with time. You could begin by acknowledging that you're not a perpetual motion machine. A computer might run around the clock. You're not a computer. You aren't made for constant motion, constant work, constant activity. You can't work twenty-four hours a day. You might manage it for a day or two, but it will come at a high cost.

Life is about cycles. The old saying reminds you that "you are a human being not a human doing." Life is more than doing. It's also about being. As a human being you need—really need—to alternate work and play, activity and rest, wakefulness and sleep.

Enjoying Your Relationship with Time

Your relationship with time is a critical aspect of what it means to live your life creatively and happily. As long as you're constantly doing and not allowing enough time to be, you'll be chronically dissatisfied with yourself because you aren't doing enough. Because you don't have enough time, you have to rush and multitask and give up the activities that you used to love. You'll be constantly peeved because other people aren't doing things fast enough. Or you'll be on the receiving end of the complaints of unhappy people around you that you aren't doing enough fast enough.

Kipling's words about "filling the unforgiving minute with sixty seconds worth of distance run" summarize the pervasive belief that you have to keep moving. If you stop moving, you're "wasting time." By this definition, wasting time is any time that isn't spent doing what you "have to do."

A better guide than Kipling's words are these words by Carl Bard:

> Though no one can go back and make a brand new start, anyone can start from now and make a brand new ending.

Your brand new ending relates directly to your beliefs about time. It begins by recognizing that time is precious and that it deserves your best use of it. It doesn't mean running a race all the time. It means savoring the time you have.

Let's redefine the notion of "wasting time." Consider these words by Bertrand Russell:

> The time you enjoy wasting is not wasted time.

You can consider this as an absurd oxymoron—or you can recognize these words as a liberating insight into how to live a full, creative, satisfying life by adding the verb *enjoy* to your thoughts about time.

It's true that your time on this Earth is limited. No one has enough time to do *everything*. That doesn't mean that you don't have time to enjoy living your life. The key word here is *enjoy*. The word is derived from Latin by way of Old French. It means to *give joy, to take delight in, to rejoice.* Joy is *a feeling of pleasure, delight, and happiness*. A stressed-out life is a life without joy.

These words challenge the idea that you have so much to do that you can't take any time to enjoy yourself. That you need to do more, work more, get more done. My husband's mother used to tell him: "You have to get your work done before you can go out and play." It's one thing to require a child to finish work before going out to play. "Get your work done before you play" is another matter for adults.

The reality of our contemporary adult lives is that the work is never done. Your stressed-out self will tell you that you don't have time to play. "Play" means more than playing some sort of organized game—whether it's a sport or a card game. Adults have a way of turning sports and games into contests rather than activities that are fun. This kind of playing becomes one more stress-inducing activity rather than an opportunity to experience joy.

TIME AND YOUR WELLBEING

You develop a different perspective on time by setting your own priorities about how you use it. The essential element is *focus*. You focus on what's important to you, what you choose to do, and how you're going to do it.

How much of what you do contributes to your sense of peace, wellbeing, and joy? Many people who feel constantly stressed-out are working hard without recognizing that the real cause of their stress is that they aren't doing enough of the right kinds of activities. Marcus Buckingham says it well:

> Many of us feel stress and get overwhelmed not because we're taking on too much, but because we're taking on too little of what really strengthens us.

Maybe you're feeling stressed-out because you aren't strengthening yourself with activities that nurture you. Sometimes the missing piece is doing more rather than doing less. By this I don't mean the default idea of getting a massage or taking a long, lingering bubble bath "to relieve your stress."

Maybe what you really crave is a hike in the mountains. Maybe you're eager to act in a play or to paint a picture. Maybe you're not reading enough books. Maybe you'd like to play your long-neglected guitar. Maybe you're not spending enough time in conversations with friends that are about life and joy and laughter. Maybe you're feeling so stressed-out because you never seem to have enough time to travel or ride a horse or go on a photo shoot—or anything else you would love to do.

WHAT WOULD YOU LOVE TO DO?

What compromises are you making in your life to do what you think you must do? What did you love to do that you don't do anymore because you "don't have time." What life-enriching activities gave you great pleasure before you became so responsible? What *don't* you do to take on the endless responsibilities of work, family, job, career, business, and social groups?

Consider how much you're giving up to maintain your current schedule. How much have you traded something you love for something you don't care about? When you stop "wasting time" doing what gives you joy, you begin a decline into a state of mind where you're nothing more than a human machine doing assigned tasks.

In other words, what have you sacrificed that matters to you in the service of what does not matter to you? Every decision you make is a decision not to do anything else. Is the trade is worth the cost? Do you have to give up doing what nurtures you, energizes you, delights you? Do you have to give up what you love to meet someone else's expectations?

Life is full of choices. Are the choices you made worth the time of your life? Whatever choices you have made throughout your life, you can take Carl Bard's words to heart. You can't start over but you can start from now and make your brand new ending.

~

Questions to Think About

1. How do your thoughts about time create stress in your life?

2. What do you think about wasting time?

3. What are you doing that you don't care about?

4. What aren't you doing that you do care about?

5. Do you attempt to multitask? How does multitasking affect your focus?

6. Has it become a badge of honor for you to be stressed-out?

7. How can you enjoy your relationship with time?

8. How can you follow Carl Bard's words of wisdom and make a brand new ending?

9. What do you think of Marcus Buckingham's claim that "many of us feel stress and get overwhelmed not because we're taking on too much, but because we're taking on too little of what really strengthens us"?

10. What would you love to do if you had more time?

Chapter 8

Thinking About
Stress and Enough

Gratitude unlocks the fullness of life. It turns what we have into enough, and more. It turns denial into acceptance, chaos to order, confusion to clarity. It can turn a meal into a feast, a house into a home, a stranger into a friend. Gratitude makes sense of our past, brings peace for today, and creates a vision for tomorrow.

Melody Beatty

STRESS AND ENOUGH

The promise of abundance defines much New Age self-help work. According to this promise, you can have unlimited abundance if you develop the right mindset. One example of such claims about abundance is this assessment by Ben Sweetland:

The world is full of abundance and opportunity, but far too many people come to the fountain of life with a sieve instead of a tank car—a teaspoon instead of a steam shovel. They expect little and as a result they get little.

Rather than consider the how-tos of acquiring abundance, let's focus on a different question by substituting *enough* for *abundance*. The question then becomes:

> How does your perception of *enough* relate to whether you feel stressed-out or peaceful?

Why substitute *enough* for *abundance*? Although the concept of *abundance* is wonderful to contemplate, the word *enough* holds a significant clue about how to transform a stressed-out life into a peaceful life. Simply talking about abundance in your life doesn't require you to identify how much abundance is *enough* for you to "tame" your stressed-out emotions.

Enough is a word that isn't used enough. *Enough* sets the boundaries. What's *enough* for you to be happy? What's *enough* for you to feel secure? What's *enough* for you to feel successful? What's *enough* to end your stressed-out feelings concerning money?

Stressed-out demonstrates an imbalance between *more* and *less,* between *too much* and *too little, too many* and *too few.* You might be saying that you have *too much* to do, which is another way of saying that you have *too little* time to do it. You owe *more* in bills, which means you have *less* money than you need to pay them. You have *too much* responsibility and *too little* help. *Too much* work means *too little* play. *Too* exhausted means *less* sleep than you need. *Too* tense means *too little* relaxation. However you express it, your stressed-out state of mind reveals that something is out of balance in your life. You think you don't have *enough* to feel peaceful.

WHAT IS ENOUGH?

Let's look more carefully at the idea of *enough*. Does "enough" mean just enough to scrape by? One of the phrases I heard throughout my childhood was "make do with what you have." This definition was a legacy of the Great Depression and World War II. During the war, government posters encouraged frugality with this phrase:

Use it Up, Wear it Out, Make it Do, or Do Without

Making do substituted something of inferior quality because the real thing was not available. Other phrases include *"making ends meet, keeping your head above water, make the best of, get by, manage, cope, survive, keep the wolf from the door.*

Consider what Oprah Winfrey claims about this meaning of enough:

Be thankful for what you have; you'll end up having more. If you concentrate on what you don't have, you will never, ever have enough.

The *enough* of "making do" demonstrates a scarcity mindset of limitation and lack. This stress-inducing meaning of *enough* cannot create a peaceful life

NEVER ENOUGH

On the other end of the *what's enough* spectrum, some people never have *enough* no matter how much they have. This *never enough* perspective is often a legacy of people who grew up learning how to *make do.* They can become financially successful but never feel financially secure. For them, no amount of abundance is enough.

Such people often become what the French name *nouveau riche.* The English equivalent is *new rich* or *new money.* The terms are often used as pejoratives to describe people who show off their newly acquired wealth in contrast to *old money* people who grew up rich and don't feel the need to show off their wealth. Many of these new rich have a lot of money but never quite reach the point of feeling that they have enough.

I know of one such person who became very wealthy very quickly. He discovered that another newly-rich acquaintance had a house with a walk-in closet in the bedroom that was bigger than the living room in his own house. Suddenly, his house was not big enough. He had to buy a much bigger house so he too could have a huge closet in a huge bedroom.

The ancient Greek philosopher Epicurus described this kind of reaction in these words:

> Nothing is enough for the man to whom enough is too little.

This definition of *enough* is still about a stress-inducing perception of lack and limitation. If you have a similar story to tell, you might have an abundance of money in the bank and be able to buy just about anything you want, all the while feeling that you don't have enough. You need more. Always more.

TOO MANY OPTIONS

Consider also the experience of stress created by *too much*. Stressed-out is a feeling that you can't cope, can't keep up, can't do all that's expected of you, all that's required of you, all that you want to do.

A powerful cause of much contemporary stress is an overabundance of options. One of the realities of living in the era we do is that we have so many choices for so many things. Way back when, if you wanted toothpaste, you might have three or four choices. Now you have a whole aisle of choices. It's the same with just about everything. More choices means more time selecting what you want. More and more and more.

Human beings never had such abundance of choices before our era. In this respect—although not in so many other ways—life was easier for our forebears who weren't exposed to endless advertising about such a vast array of *stuff*. It's wonderful to have so any options and it's also a trap. More options require more choices. Sometimes, ignorance really is bliss.

WANTING MORE

The whole purpose of advertising is to get you to *want* things. *Want* means both *lack* and *desire*. The better the ad, the more you want what the ad offers. You covet it. If you didn't know about something, you wouldn't feel lack by not having it.

You know how it is. Someone shows you the latest gizmo, or you see a demonstration of a gadget in a store, or you see something on TV, and suddenly, you must have this new thing.

More options mean more pressure to choose between them or to attempt to acquire them. The more options, the more choices, the more to do, the more stress when you can't have it all or, do it all, get or it all done.

Meanwhile, everything you use changes relentlessly. The futurist Alvin Toffler identified the experience in his internationally best-selling book, *Future Shock*, published in 1970. He defined *future shock* as:

> Too much change in too short a period of time.

In his later books, he continued to identify the stress-inducing realities of living in a world that is undergoing constant, relentless, stress-inducing change:

> The illiterate of the 21st century will not be those who cannot read and write, but those who cannot learn, unlearn, and relearn.

UPDATING

Future shock has become a way of life as we are required to learn, unlearn, and relearn just about everything we do. We spend a lot of time learning and unlearning and relearning how to use the essential tools of twenty-first century life. It used to be that if you had a hammer, you learned to use it. Over time, you became a master at using your hammer. You didn't have to "update" your hammer frequently and then learn how to use your new hammer.

Now, the tools you use in your life are frequently "updated" to provide a whole new user experience. You might discover that you spend about as much time updating your tools as you do using them.

If you maintain a website, you know what it's like. Updates. New editions. New programs. You install the update and then discover that your website now has a conflict between programs. So you spend time fixing that rather than doing whatever you intended to do on your computer.

Even if you don't have your own website, you might discover that paying your bills online can be a challenge. You log into your account to pay your bill and discover that the vendor site has been "updated" since the last time you paid a bill. Now you have to figure out how to navigate the revised site with all of its new features. You no doubt have your own examples of being sidetracked from doing what you intended to do because your technology changed and you had to figure out how to use it.

Using a telephone has also become a high art. In the olden days of telephones, you picked up a receiver and spoke to an operator. You didn't need a manual to do that. Now your telephone has metamorphosed into a technological wonder. Your phone now comes with a user's manual in multiple languages that's supposed to explain all of the features and how to use them. Among other features, you can read books, pay bills, take pictures, play games, and visit websites. You can even talk to someone else on your updated, upgraded, twenty-first century telephone.

FOCUSED THOUGHT

How do you cope with all of this change in too short a time? You can use the most powerful tool you have—the capacity to think. Napoleon Hill titled his classic book *Think and Grow Rich*. He claimed that "thoughts are things." Thoughts create the means of wealth. This doesn't mean that you can think about money and that suddenly piles of cash will appear before you. Creation of wealth is not about mumbo jumbo, incantations and rituals, or magic words. For Hill, the thinking leads to action and the action results in the creation of "things" that produce wealth.

The power of thought derives from sustained focus. You concentrate your thought on what you desire to do and to have. Your ability to maintain focus on what matters to you is directly related to your ability to create abundance in your life.

One of the defining characteristics of highly successful people is their ability to focus on what matters without being distracted by what doesn't matter to them. Such people can go into a restaurant, scan the menu briefly, and decide quickly. Meanwhile other diners spend a long time looking at the options and asking other people at the table what they are going to order before they choose an option on the menu.

How Do You Spend Your Thoughts?

If you're feeling stressed-out by not having enough time or money or resources to live the life you desire to live, you can pay attention to how you *spend your thoughts* thinking about minor matters. If the idea that you spend thoughts seems a bit strange, you can play a little game with yourself. Put a price tag on your thoughts. Let's keep the cost low and say that you decide that every minute of thought is worth one dollar—or whatever unit of currency you use. So, if you spend thirty minutes of your time reading labels as you ponder what toothpaste to buy, the cost of thirty minutes of your time adds up to $30. That doesn't cover the actual cost you pay for the toothpaste.

Let's keep the math easy and say that the toothpaste costs $5. That means you pay $5 for the toothpaste and $30 for the time you spent choosing the toothpaste. That's one expensive tube of toothpaste.

Your decision to focus on what matters and not get bogged on less important choices allows you to concentrate on creating what you care about. Ask yourself if it's worth your time to spend thirty minutes in the toothpaste aisle reading labels before you decide what toothpaste to buy.

The key to all of this is focus. If you focus on lack and doing without and eking by, you'll continue to experience lack no matter how much money you have. If you focus your thoughts on creating enough to experience abundance, you'll expand how you think about your life.

At the very least, focusing on what you intend to create, to have, and to be transforms stressed-out into peaceful. Stress results from feeling squeezed, compressed, and limited. When you feel stressed-out, you're thinking from your *lower brain*—your brain stem, which is also known as the reptilian brain. Your lower brain focuses on survival. You can't think higher thoughts from your lower brain. However, if you change your focus from *lack* to *enough,* you can think thoughts of abundance rather than scarcity. When you're thinking with your *higher brain*—your pre-frontal cortex—you can transform stress thoughts into success thoughts.

ABUNDANCE AND GRATITUDE

Abundance teaching consistently emphasizes the connection between gratitude and abundance. Zig Ziglar coined the phrase: "Have an attitude of gratitude." He claimed:

The more you recognize and express gratitude for the things you have, the more things you will have to express gratitude for.

It's easy to get cynical about clever "attitude of gratitude" language when it's spoken as a celebration of a particular person's wealth and fortune. It sounds too good to be true and doesn't feel very helpful when you're barely scraping by in life. However, the transformative power of these words relates directly to your perception of how much abundance you need to have enough.

Remember the words of Epicurus: "Nothing is enough for the man to whom enough is too little." If enough is too little for you, you're unlikely to have an attitude of gratitude for what you do have.

Gratitude also relates directly your experience of stress. Zig Ziglar also said this:

Without gratitude, happiness is rare. With gratitude, the odds for happiness go up dramatically.

Happy people are not stressed-out people. An attitude of gratitude begins with thankfulness for what you do have. It's difficult to be simultaneously grateful and stressed-out at the same time. Stress squeezes your perception of your life. The more compressed you feel, the fewer choices you think you have, the less you think you have, the more you feel stressed-out.

DID YOU SEE THE GORILLA?

Focus increases your awareness of what you have. You see what you focus upon. If you aren't looking for something, you might not see it, even if it's right before your eyes. If you doubt this, consider this demonstration I observed at a seminar I attended several years ago.

The seminar leader told us that we were going to see a video of two three-person teams of basketball players who were passing balls between each other. Our task was to count the number of times the ball was passed between the players wearing white shirts. We watched and counted. I remember that we watched the video twice. At one point in the second viewing, I glimpsed a moving shadow, but otherwise, I saw nothing except basketball players passing balls between each other.

After the second viewing, the leader asked if any of us had observed something else in the video. As I remember, only two or three people among several hundred raised their hands. He then asked how many of us had seen the gorilla. Then he played the video again. This time, I saw a person in a gorilla suit slowly moving between the players.

WHAT DON'T YOU SEE?

Consider the implications. Several hundred people watched a video two times, concentrating on counting the number of passes between the players. Almost all of us didn't see what was right before our eyes. (And maybe the few people who did see it had already seen the video.) The closest I came to seeing the gorilla was that fleeting glimpse of what looked like a shadow. When we were told about the gorilla, the gorilla suddenly became visible. It was there all the time, but most of us didn't see it because we were counting how many times the white shirt team passed the basketball. We didn't see the gorilla because we weren't looking for it.

If you've never seen this video, you can watch it yourself. (The link is in the note.) Since you know about the gorilla, you'll surely see the gorilla. You might find it hard to believe that almost all of us didn't see it because we were paying attention to counting the passes between the players in white shirts.[20]

Consider the implications for your perceptions concerning abundance. If you're focused on lack, you'll see only lack. If you aren't looking for abundance in your life, you probably won't see it, even if abundance is right in front of you. However, if you look for abundance in your life, you'll see abundance.

Relate this to Deborah Norville's claim:

> If you consciously take note of what is good in your life, quantifiable benefits happen.

GRATITUDE AS A WEAPON AGAINST STRESS

Gratitude for what you have is a powerful weapon against stressed-out thoughts. Gratitude expands constriction into room to breathe by expressing the belief that you will have enough, even if you don't have it now. Gratitude creates an interactive feedback loop. The more gratitude you feel and express, the more your attitude changes to be positive and uplifting. The more your attitude changes, the more gratitude you feel.

Abundance is a state of mind as much as it a copious amount of something. People can and do create massive amounts of wealth. They can have an abundance of every kind of material good there is, and still not be satisfied. The big house is not big enough, because someone else has a bigger house. This is not the attitude of abundance. If you measure abundance by comparing yourself to someone else, you will never have enough.

Words can express gratitude for abundance. Words can also express your complaints about what you lack. As you listen to your own words about your life, what do you hear? How does your language relate to your experience of abundance or lack, of peacefulness or stressed-out? Are you complaining about what you don't have or expressing gratitude for what you do have? Do your words express only lack, only wanting, only limitation? Do your words express abundance, thankfulness, appreciation? Whatever you believe or don't believe about religious or spiritual claims about prayer, expressing your gratitude in words has power to change your perspective on your life.

Gratitude for *anything* in your life is a change in perspective from a mindset of lack. If you're feeling very discouraged by your life, find something you're truly grateful to have and express that gratitude in words. If you feel that you don't have enough of anything in your life, you can make Melody Beatty's words your own:

> Gratitude unlocks the fullness of life. It turns what we have into enough, and more. It turns denial into acceptance, chaos to order, confusion to clarity. It can turn a meal into a feast, a house into a home, a stranger into a friend. Gratitude makes sense of our past, brings peace for today, and creates a vision for tomorrow.

~

QUESTIONS TO THINK ABOUT

1. How does your perception of enough relate to whether you feel stressed-out or peaceful?

2. What's enough for you to be happy?

3. What's enough for you to feel secure?

4. What's enough for you to feel successful?

5. What's enough to end your stressed-out feelings concerning money?

6. How do you relate to the words by Epicurus that "nothing is enough for the man to whom enough is too little"?

7. Do you feel stressed-out by too much?

8. Do you feel that there's too much change in too short a period of time?

9. How well do you maintain focus on what matters to you?

10. Do you spend your thoughts thinking about minor matters?

11. How does gratitude relate to your experience of stress?

12. Did you see the gorilla in the video? What does this video demonstrate about focus in your life?

Chapter 9

Thinking About
Stress and Your Past

The worst pain isn't the pain you feel at the time, it's the pain you feel later on when there's nothing you can do about it. They say that time heals all wounds, but we never live long enough to test that theory.

José Saramago

STRESS AND YOUR PAST

What's the connection between your current stressed-out state of mind and your life history? If you've done any sort of personal development work, you've probably heard that you must *let go* of the hurts and pains of your past to be free. Here are three examples of such counsel:

Deepak Chopra claims:

In the process of letting go you will lose many things from the past, but you will find yourself.

Mary Manin Morrissey claims:

Even though you may want to move forward in your life, you may have one foot on the brakes. In order to be free, we must learn how to let go. Release the hurt. Release the fear. Refuse to entertain your old pain. The energy it takes to hang onto the past is holding you back from a new life. What is it you would let go of today?

Jack Kornfield claims:

> To let go is to release the images and emotions, the grudges and fears, the clinging and disappointments of the past that bind our spirit.

Let's begin by acknowledging the wisdom of these three claims about letting go of the pains, hurts, and fears that bind you to the past and blind you to other possibilities for your future. You can't move forward if you're chained to the past just as a thoroughbred racehorse chained to the starting gate can't move forward when the bell rings.

The words "let go" express the belief that you can set yourself free by deciding to be free. You might have heard, read about, or even seen a demonstration that letting go is as simple as letting go of the pen you're gripping tightly in your hand. "Just release your grip. Tip your hand to the side. Let the pen fall to the floor." It sounds simple enough. Just let it go. However, letting go of the pains of your past is not as easy as letting a pen fall to the floor.

RESISTANCE TO LETTING GO

Consider this statement by Thich Nhat Hanh concerning resistance to letting go:

> People have a hard time letting go of their suffering. Out of a fear of the unknown, they prefer suffering that is familiar.

The astonishing verb choice "prefer" captures both the essence of what so many self-help teachers say about resistance to letting go and why such language is so tone-deaf concerning people who are stuck in suffering as a result of traumatic experiences.

If you consider these words according the root meaning of the word *resistance*, Thich Nhat Hanh claims that resistant people are taking a firm stand in opposition to letting go of their suffering. Why would suffering people do that? Do they really "prefer" suffering that is familiar because they're afraid of the unknown?

Let's consider the claim that someone "prefers suffering" because it's familiar. The root meaning of the word *prefer* is "to put before." Usage can range from formal usage such as "preferring charges" in a court of law to informal language about liking something more than something else. In common speech, you might say that you prefer chocolate ice cream rather than vanilla, coffee rather than tea, and baseball rather than basketball.

The significant question is: What exactly are you supposed to let go? Your feelings? Your memories? Your identity? Deepak Chopra has no list, just the assertion that you will find your self if you let go of *things from the past*. Mary Manin Morrissey's list includes *hurt, fear,* and *pain.* Jack Kornfield's list includes *images, emotions, grudges, fears, clinging,* and *disappointments.* A list of words doesn't do justice to the power of these words as lived experiences. As words without context, it's all theoretical. These statements also omit the most stress-inducing word of all—*trauma.*

TRAUMA

Letting go of a pen in your hand has value as an analogy. However, for someone who has experienced life-altering trauma, this simplistic analogy isn't much help and can actually cause you to feel worse about yourself.

Trauma—real life-changing trauma—can affect you in ways that become deeply engrained in your sense of identity, your body, and your brain. Trauma changes you. Traumas are powerful stressors that can produce post-traumatic stress disorder (PTSD). The stress resulting from PTSD doesn't go away by simply deciding to let it go. The combination of helplessness and fear for your life can endure for a lifetime. If you experienced trauma, "just let go" is not only too simplistic to be of much use, it can also reinforce your own sense of helplessness. Using the language of preference to describe someone stuck in a state of post-traumatic stress demonstrates extraordinary lack of compassion for the one who suffers. People with post-traumatic stress disorder don't *prefer* to feel that way.

A pen is not part of you. It never was part of you. It never will be part of you. In contrast, the traumas of the past are part of you. They're deeply rooted in memory. Your mind remembers. Your body remembers. Your brain remembers.

Traumas leave scars—whether visible or invisible. The invisible scars hurt the most. You can see it in combat veterans who come back from war with post-traumatic stress disorder. The war might over, but the battle never stops.

Most people wouldn't say to someone whose body was scarred by some sort of trauma, "Let go of your scar." They wouldn't say it because they know that the scar has become part of the wounded body. It might be possible for a plastic surgeon to remove the scar—or maybe not. In either case, getting rid of the scar is not as simple as letting go of a pen in your hand.

CONFRONTING PAIN

Suffering people don't resist because they prefer to suffer. Rather, they resist because they're in pain. Bell Hooks claims:

> True resistance begins with people confronting pain and wanting to do something to change it.

Hal Zina Bennett's description of essential wounds gets to the heart of the matter. Essential wounds are wounds to your essence—your being. When you're wounded in some way, your perception of who you are as a human being is challenged:

> We make sense of the world through creating inner pictures of what our lives are about. Usually these pictures more or less work, so we're justified in believing in them, in depending on them. Then something happens that pushes the limits, that reminds us we have fabricated these pictures out of our limited view of what makes the universe tick. What's more, we can't always depend on other people—even our loved ones—to comfort or protect us, or even to see our needs, when the pictures fail us.[21]

These words claim that your suffering is not so much about the original traumatic experience itself, but about your perception of your world. Will anyone listen? Do the people you tell believe you? Do they care? The essential wound results when the people you tell don't listen, don't care, and don't believe you. They minimize the traumatic harm you experienced with simplistic statements such as "Let it go. Get over it. Move on." When you want someone to listen and to care, those who minimize your suffering are in effect telling you that the pain of your life doesn't matter very much.

WHY YOU RESIST

Resistance is about taking a stand against something. Whatever the "something" is, you refuse to do it, you remain strong against some force, or you prevent yourself from doing something that you want to do. In other words, resistance acts like a potent counterbalance to just about anything that's going on in your life. It's yin against yang, it's push against pull, it's no against yes, it's gravity pulling you down when you jump up. Resistance is with you always. No matter what you're doing, something or someone is exerting force on you to do the opposite.

It's true that you can be the source of your greatest resistance. Why are you so resistant to letting go of old stories, old beliefs, old ways of thinking, old ways of talking? If we leave aside the unhelpful notion that you "prefer to suffer" rather than change your life for the better, we can consider the most powerful reason that you resist letting go.

You know what your life is like now. What happens if you make changes? What will you lose? Even worse, what will you bring down upon yourself? Even if you've been longing to do something and you finally get the opportunity to do it, you're reluctant to let go of your past.

Even the thought of change triggers resistance. Resistance is the inner counterweight that tries to keep you where you are. If you think about doing something beyond your usual routine, resistance tells you not to do it. Underneath it all, your resistance is trying to protect you. Sometimes, resistance gets it right. Resistance can keep you from making rash decisions, telling you to think it through before you invest your life savings in the latest get-rich-quick scheme. Sometimes, resistance gets it wrong. This is when resistance becomes the well-meaning, over-protective parent who wants to keep you safe by preventing you from doing anything that might harm you. You become the child who stands at the window watching other children ride their dangerous bikes. You won't get hurt falling off a bike because you aren't allowed to ride one.

Whatever you're doing or not doing, your inner resistance pushes you in the opposite direction. You're tired of your familiar routine day in and day out. You resist the sameness of it all. At the same time, you resist any efforts to change your routine, to let go of the familiar, to try something new. When you think of doing something else, you can count on resistance to tell you to stay put.

FEAR

The greatest weapon resistance uses against you is fear. Fear is a typical response to what is unknown. Fear of what you will encounter. Fear of what will happen to you. Fear of dangers that lurk beyond your knowing. Fear of what might happen if you fail. Fear of what might happen if you succeed.

You also remember the fears of the traumatic experiences of your past. Resistance is a protection mechanism. If you experienced life-threatening trauma in your life—whether it was some sudden injury, experience in combat, a crime committed against you, abuse within a toxic family, or any other kind of traumatic experience—you were both afraid and hurt. The traumas of the past affected you deeply. Your resistance is doing everything it can to protect you from further harm.

Fear of future life-threatening harm, based on past traumatic experiences, produces strong resistance to change. Advice about letting go often lacks compassionate awareness of this fear. Telling you to simply "let go" of your memories of trauma without acknowledging this fear is the kind of help that is no help at all.

For such people, resistance is not "fear of the unknown" but fear of something far more basic—the fear of death. You think this is exaggerated? It only seems exaggerated for anyone who has never experienced such fear. Is it logical? Rational? A fear that can be as easily released as letting a pen roll off your hand? Such fears are deeply rooted in your body and your mind. They don't easily surrender to commands to let go.

LETTING GO OF WHAT?

Part of the complexity of the idea of letting go is the question: What exactly are you letting go? Is it the same as cutting off a burned piece of toast? Is it the same as cutting off a burned leg—the leg that the doctors tell you they cannot save and that will cause your death if they don't amputate immediately?

What if the injuries are not as visible as burned toast or a burned leg? What if your injuries involved betrayal of trust? What if you were tormented, raped, beaten, or starved? What if you were in combat and saw horrors that you'll never forget? Even if there are no visible scars of such experiences, such experiences leave invisible wounds that are not easily let go.

Ask yourself this significant question: What exactly are you supposed to let go? It's one thing to say to someone: "It's time to throw away the old sweater with holes in the elbows." It's another to say: "Throw away your memories." It's easy enough for someone to tell you to forget about it, to put it behind you, and move on. But, you can't forget your own life so easily. Your resistance to change is not because you love to suffer, but because you aren't willing to let go of your past because your past is yours. If you let go of your past, what do you have left?

DOES YOUR LIFE MATTER?

In such circumstances, when you're told to "let go" by people who do not know what you experienced and aren't willing to listen long enough to find out, you're being told to betray your traumatic truth, your own painful history, and to act as if it didn't matter all that much.

Some self-help teaching says as much. The idea of "letting go" is deeply rooted in Eastern philosophical traditions that claim that your perception that you're a separate entity from the One is an illusion. Western New Age ideologies based on Eastern philosophical tradition, such as *The Course in Miracles,* claim that the "real you"—the perfect you—was never harmed.

As a result, the attitude of such New Age teachers who have not yet mastered compassion seems to be something like this:

> Since you—the real you—can't be harmed, why are you upset? The real you was never harmed. The "you" who thinks you were hurt is an illusion. So get over yourself already. Just let go.

If you think I'm making this up, I assure that I have actually heard or read such statements by some New Age teachers in various classes I attended and in books I read. Some even go far as to claim that if you were hurt, you must have *wanted* to be hurt—to experience what that felt like. In other words, you *caused* your own suffering so you could experience what suffering feels like.

The idea of "letting go" can easily turn into this kind of simplistic thinking about how to heal what hurt you so deeply. It begins with the assumption that whatever happened to you doesn't matter in the grand scheme of things—because "the real you" was never hurt—or that you somehow "chose" your experience. In other words, it's not much help if you're suffering.

The Value of Your Life

Let's go to a deeper place than telling you to let go of your emotional responses to painful experiences. Let's consider the value of your own life. The deepest wound of any traumatic experience comes down to the value of your life. You deserve your life. Why? Because you're alive. You deserve to be treated well. Why? Because you're alive. You don't have to do anything to deserve being treated well.

Recent tragic events have brought to American national consciousness the phrase, "Black lives matter." Black lives do matter. So does your life—whatever your skin color. Your life matters. Your emotional responses to the harm done to you express your own belief that your life matters. If you were abused, and no one seemed to care, you learned that other people thought you weren't worthy of being treated well.

From this perspective, your resistance to letting go is not about fear of the future, but an effort to assert the value of your life. Consider these propositions:

- If you feel angry, it's because you're angry at the harm someone did to you.
- If you're anxious, it's because you're afraid it will happen to you again.
- If you're carrying a grudge, it's because someone hurt you and has never expressed remorse or held responsible.
- If you feel pain, it's because you still hurt.

These are responses rather than causes. They're symptoms of being treated as if your life doesn't matter. Rather than try to let go of your emotions about whatever happened to you, a better place to begin is by changing your thoughts about the value of your life as a human being.

THREE TRUTHS

How do you both reclaim the value of your life and move beyond the stuckness of trauma? You can begin by acknowledging three truths:

- You were deeply hurt.
- You can reclaim the value of your life.
- You can change your brain, your body, and your thoughts.

If you were badly treated and no one seems to care, it's up to you to reclaim the value of your life. You get there by finding a different way to measure your own value. You can begin to change your thoughts with this question:

> If you were mistreated, injured, or harmed in ways that you can't seem to get beyond, are you going to allow this experience to define your value as a human being for the rest of your life?

Instead of thinking of yourself as someone whose life doesn't matter enough to be treated well, you declare to yourself that your life does matter. You also declare to yourself that you are more than the injury. You are more than the abuse. You are more than your past hurts, traumas, anxieties, and fears.

The truth is that you already believe that your life matters. That's why you feel so hurt. You were mistreated—perhaps you're still being mistreated—and no one around you seems to care. Compassion-free simplistic statements telling you to "just let go" imply that whatever happened to you didn't matter all that much because *you* don't matter that all that much.

What's the connection between letting go and acknowledging the value of your own life. It comes down to the question, "Does your life matter or not?" What's the value of your life if you have been traumatized, wounded, abused, hurt, or otherwise, treated badly? This leads to the disconnection between the simplicity of being told to let go and the urge within you to scream out to the world: "Does it matter to you that I was so badly hurt?"

If you believed that your life doesn't matter, you wouldn't mind being treated as human garbage, or someone's punching bag, or target of abuse. You feel what you feel because you believe you deserve better than that.

People without compassion are very quick to minimize your suffering. In the process, they minimize the value of your life and they deny you the opportunity to tell your truth about how the experience hurt you. They'll tell you to let go without allowing you to grieve what you experienced.

I suspect that one of the great obstacles to letting go, especially when people use the words so glibly—"just let go"—is that letting go feels like self-betrayal. However terrible they are, your memories are your memories. When you get rid of them, you get rid of part of you. You get rid of what you experienced. It's like lopping off your right arm because it hurts. It hurts, but it's the only right arm you have.

You're reluctant to let go because letting go means obliterating a part of your life experience.

The aftermath of trauma is like being on a moving walkway that's turned off. If you're stuck in trauma, it's time to turn on the walkway. Whatever happened to you, you're more than a traumatized person. You can put the pieces together and move forward to become whole again.

~

QUESTIONS TO THINK ABOUT

1. What's the connection between your current stressed-out state of mind and your life history?
2. Are you resistant to letting go of the pain of your past?
3. Do you have painful memories of trauma?
4. How do you relate to what Hal Zina Bennett claims about essential wounds?
5. Are you resistant to change because you aren't willing to let go of your past?
6. How do you feel when people minimize what happened to you?
7. How do you both reclaim the value of your life and move beyond the stuckness of trauma?
8. If you were mistreated, injured, or harmed in ways that you can't seem to get beyond, are you going to allow this experience to define your value as a human being for the rest of your life?

Chapter 10

Thinking About
Stress and Your Future

Holding on is believing that there's only a past;
letting go is knowing that there's a future.

Daphne Rose Kingma

STRESS AND YOUR FUTURE

The words of Daphne Rose Kingma identify the missing piece in so many simplistic admonitions to "just let go."

Think of the adventure stories when an Indiana Jones-type hero tries to escape a horde of spear-carrying natives running behind him. Suddenly he comes to a deep, narrow crevice between two high cliffs. He has to get across the crevice to escape the natives. How does he get to the other side? He grabs hold of a conveniently located vine hanging down the face of the cliff. He swings across the deep rift in the rocks but the vine isn't long enough to get him to the other side. The vine swings him back to the edge of the crevice.

He hears the yelling of the natives close behind him. Then he sees a spindly tree growing out of the cliff on the other side of the crevice. A branch of the tree stretches part way across the deep gap between the cliffs. He grips the vine and swings across the crevice one more time. He grabs the branch and he lets go of the vine. The scraggly tree sags from his weight. It's pulling out of the rock cliff! Will it hold as he pulls himself along the branch to get to the top of the cliff? It does! He stands safely on the cliff. Just then, the angry natives arrive on the opposite side of the cliff. The first one grabs a vine to swing across. Our hero pushes the tree into the deep crevasse. The natives cannot follow him. He has escaped.

How many times have you seen something like this in adventure movies, comic books, and cartoons? The hero gets where he wants to go by letting go of one thing and grabbing hold of something else.

Let's change the story a bit. Our hero is on one side of the cliff. The spear-carrying natives are close behind. On the opposite cliff, the hero's mentors, teachers, family, and friends stand watching. He grabs hold of the vine and makes his first effort to swing across. The vine isn't long enough to reach to the other side. The vine swings him back to where he was. He stands on the side of the cliff, not knowing what to do. Then his mentors, teachers, and friends take on the role of a Greek chorus as they chant, "let go, let go, let go, let go, let go." He grabs the vine. He leaps forward. Halfway across, he lets go of the vine. He falls to his certain death. End of story.

SOMETHING TO GRAB ONTO

This is the missing piece in simplistic admonitions to "let go." If you let go, what do you grab onto? The fear of letting go is related to a fear of falling—a fear that's typical of most humans and mammals. Letting go of the past isn't literally equivalent to falling off a cliff. However letting go of the past is metaphorically equivalent to falling off a cliff.

Whether you take it literally or metaphorically, "just let go" isn't enough to free yourself from whatever is holding you back. You need something to grab onto. In Daphne Rose Kingma's words, "Letting go is knowing that there's a future." The essential element needed for letting go of the grip of trauma over you is to have a vision of a better future.

"Just let go" has no vision of your future. Vision is when you see beyond your current circumstances to imagine a life shaped by love rather than fear, peacefulness rather than stress, wholeness rather than fragmentation. This vision is essential to overcoming your resistance to letting go of the fears and beliefs that bind you to your past.

One of the most life-changing experiences of my own life was a vision of a different possibility for my future when I was seven years old. My vision for the future began with a color illustration in a second grade reading book. The picture showed Alice and Jerry, with their dog, Jip, running with open arms to their father. The father was in the foreground of the picture with his arms stretched out.

I can't over-exaggerate the importance of that picture in my life. It showed me an alternative vision, a possibility for a different life than anything I had ever experienced. I never ran to the open arms of my father, for the simple reason that his arms were never outstretched to welcome his children. His arms were assault weapons, used to hit. If I saw him coming, I ran the other way. That color illustration was the first time I ever thought that children could be glad to see their father come home.

That image stayed with me throughout the remaining years of my childhood. It became a guiding vision in my terrified life, my hope for a better future. A single vision can do that. One glimpse of a reality that transcends anything you're currently experiencing can provide both hope and resolve to live a different life someday.

WHY HOLDING ON IS IMPORTANT

Self-help teachers often tell you to *let go* of your past. They rarely mention your need to *hold on* to your past. Havelock Ellis provides liberating wisdom about how to live a whole, happy, and peaceful life:

> All the art of living lies in a fine mingling of letting go and holding on.

A "fine mingling of letting go and holding on" allows you to remember your past and imagine your future as you live fully in the now.

Moving forward doesn't mean you forget what happened to you. Remembering is deeply rooted in human history. People make memorials to remember the dead, to remember significant events, to remember particular actions. This is why societies build memorials for soldiers who died in wars, memorials for the innocent victims of war, memorials for public figures, memorials on the graves of loved ones. These memorials declare that that the lives of these people mattered.

Each era has its slogans to evoke memory. Often they express outrage:

- Remember Lexington and Concord.
- Remember the Alamo.
- Remember the Maine.

- Remember Pearl Harbor.
- Remember 9/11.

The Holocaust Memorial in Washington D.C. includes the Remembrance Hall to remember those who died in the horror of the genocide of Jews and other "undesirable" people.[22]

These memorials are the opposite of being told to "just let go" of such memories. Rather the memorials are ways to both remember and to move forward. Life does go on. People declare that they will never forget. The ones who experienced the losses don't forget. Generations that follow won't remember because they didn't undergo the experience of loss.

YOUR PRE-TRAUMA AND POST-TRAUMA SELVES

The defining characteristic of trauma is the experience of separation. Your trauma can break you into pre-trauma and post-trauma selves. Trauma can stop the clock, stop the calendar, and stop the flow of life energy. You feel like Humpty Dumpty in the old nursery rhyme about an anthropomorphic egg:

> Humpty Dumpty sat on a wall,
>
> Humpty Dumpty had a great fall.
>
> All the king's horses and all the king's men
>
> Couldn't put Humpty together again.

The experience of trauma narrows vision, so that you can see yourself only as broken and defective. You don't know how to put the broken pieces together again.

Pain is the inevitable result of trauma. Trauma hurts. It hurts because something meant to be whole is somehow broken or fragmented. If you break a bone in your arm, the pain is the result of breaking what is meant to be unbroken. If a relationship breaks because of death, assault, unresolved conflict, betrayal, or misunderstanding, the result can be deep and unrelenting pain. Any truly traumatic experience results in pain because the trauma broke something and stopped the free flow of energy.

Throughout history, various cultures around the world have referred to the flow of energy as the essence of life itself. This flow of energy has many names. It's *qi* or *chi* or *ki* or *ch'i*. It's *prana, pneuma, mana, lüng, ruah*. It's *vital energy, energy flow, the Force*. It's *the breath of life*. Whatever this flow of energy is called, life and health involve the free flow of energy. Sickness, injury, or death results from blocked or constricted energy flow. Pain is the inevitable result of constricted energy flow. Stress and pain are inseparable companions. Both constrict the flow of energy in some way.

How does the language of letting go help you heal the pain of your trauma? The trauma itself separated you into pieces. Do you amputate the part of you that was wounded? Do you try to forget the memories? The idea that you can just "let go" reinforces the trauma. Although the advice to let go refers to feelings, such as anger, grief, and sadness, it's not that simple to separate your feelings from the parts of you that were traumatized. How do you let go of the part of you that suffered? The part of you that went through some sort of ordeal? The part of you that endured?

There's another way. Instead of attempting to let go of the part of you that's stuck in the trauma of the past, you focus on putting yourself back together again.

REMEMBERING AND RE-MEMBERING YOUR LIFE

How do you go beyond trauma to reclaim the value of your life? You re-member. The word *member* means *part*. You re-member when you put the fragments together to make yourself whole again. You see yourself as whole, rather than fragmented. You see your life as a movie rather than a snapshot frozen in time at the moment of greatest hurt. Instead of separating yourself from the wounded part, you welcome it as part of your whole life, but you don't let it define the rest of your life.

You're not Humpty Dumpty. It's impossible to put a broken egg back together again. However, you're not as fragile as an egg. You have the capacity to move beyond the stuck place, beyond the hurt, beyond the suffering. Not by forgetting—as if you could—but by remembering and re-membering to put the pieces back together to become whole again.

Stewart O'Nan claims:

> You couldn't relive your life, skipping the awful parts, without losing what made it worthwhile. You had to accept it as a whole—like the world, or the person you loved.

Holding on allows you to remember and re-member, especially if you experienced life-changing trauma. Your resistance to letting go is a reaction to simplistic claims about letting go of your past. You can't become whole by "letting go" of your memories of traumatic experiences. You can't amputate part of your past, to let go as easily as you can erase a computer file and have your memories disappear. Being told to let go by people who have no interest in knowing anything about your experience makes your experience of trauma worse. Until you both remember and re-member your past, you can't let go of its power over you.

TRAUMATIC EXPERIENCE AND YOUR IDENTITY

What's the impact of traumatic experience on your identity? Traumatic experience can so take over your identity that who you are is defined by what you endured. Even if your life is painful, it's familiar. If you "let go" of your identity defined by trauma, who will you be? Before you can let go, you need a vision of another possible identity.

Consider the prisoner in the movie, *The Shawshank Redemption.* He was an old man who had spent most of his life in prison. After decades as a prisoner, he was paroled. As a parolee, he didn't know how to live in the strange, new world he encountered on the outside. Too much had changed from the time he was jailed as a young man. In the prison, he had an identity. He was the librarian of a pitiful collection of books. Suddenly, he was thrust into the outside world, a world with automobiles—strange inventions he had never experienced before. He didn't know what to do, and more significantly, he didn't know who he was. How did he make the transition to the outside world with the new identity of parolee? He didn't. Because he couldn't imagine a future where he belonged, he could see no other option than a noose around his neck.

Trauma—life-changing trauma—gave you an identity. If you let go of the identity shaped by trauma, who will you be? Remembering and re-membering your past allow you to imagine a new future for your *whole self.* You can move beyond your identity shaped by trauma to create a new identity as a whole self, with a remembered and re-membered past and a vision of a future identity shaped by new possibilities.

You become whole again by having compassion for your own life. Underneath it all, trauma calls into question the value of your life. Trauma is made worse when people won't believe you, or when they minimize the hurt by saying it couldn't have been that bad. Trauma is also made worse when people make ideological claims that your soul wasn't hurt and so it really doesn't matter all that much, based on a belief that the life you're living is an illusion.

It's up to you to claim the power of compassion for your own life. You can hold on to your memories as you move on to create new memories that don't obliterate the past.

To be whole is to be undivided. You don't pretend that some defining experience in your life didn't happen. Rather, you include your memories into the whole image of yourself. You are all of your experiences. Nothing is insignificant and nothing is to be left off. You put the pieces back together to become whole. You remember and re-member all of you.

~

QUESTIONS TO THINK ABOUT

1. What is your vision for your future?

2. Is there some defining traumatic experience in your life that you can't get over?

3. Does the language of letting go help you heal the pain of your trauma?

4. How do you go beyond trauma to reclaim the value of your life?

5. How can you remember and re-member your past to put yourself back together again?

6. What's the impact of traumatic experience on your identity?

7. How can you have compassion for your own life?

PART IV

THINKING ABOUT
STRESS AND YOUR SELF

Chapter 11

Thinking About Your Self-Image

The person we believe ourselves to be will always act in a manner consistent with our self-image.

Brian Tracy

STRESS AND YOUR SELF-IMAGE

How much stress in your life is directly related to your self-image? An image is a picture, a visual representation of something. Self-image concerns your perception of your appearance. What do you think about your appearance? More significantly, what do you think other people think about your appearance?

Do you have "bad hair" days? You didn't do something well? An unexpected problem occurred? You got unwanted news? You can blame it on a bad hair day. The origin of this phrase is uncertain, but it seems to have originated in the United Kingdom from the words in the 1992 film, *Buffy the Vampire Slayer*, when Buffy says to the vampire:

I'm fine but you're obviously having a bad hair day.[23]

The phrase about bad hair quickly became a catchphrase for days when everything goes wrong—days when you feel completely stressed-out. On such days, your stressed-out frame of mind isn't really about hair at all. However, before we're too quick to disconnect bad days and bad hair, it's worth thinking about the relationship between how you feel and what you tell yourself about your appearance.

Although self-image is not just about appearance, what you think about the person you see in the mirror can be a powerful stressor in your life. What you see, and what you tell yourself about the person looking back at you in the mirror, can turn all of your days into bad hair days.

WHO DO YOU SEE IN THE MIRROR?

Who do you see when you look into the mirror? Are you satisfied with what you see? Do you primp and preen with pride at the person looking back at you? Or do you look in the mirror and see only flaws?

The classic story, *Snow White and the Seven Dwarfs,* tells a story about a vindictive, jealous woman and her relationship with her magic mirror:

> Queen: Slave in the magic mirror, come from the farthest space, through wind and darkness I summon thee. Speak! Let me see thy face.
> Magic Mirror: What wouldst thou know, my Queen?
> Queen: Magic Mirror on the wall, who is the fairest one of all?
> Magic Mirror: Famed is thy beauty, Majesty. But hold, a lovely maid I see. Rags cannot hide her gentle grace. Alas, she is more fair than thee.
> Queen: Alas for her! Reveal her name.

Magic Mirror: Lips red as the rose. Hair black as ebony. Skin white as snow.

Queen: Snow White![24]

The Evil Queen couldn't bear the thought that any other woman could be prettier than herself. The result was an obsessed woman determined to destroy the one who was fairer than she was.

EGO

Ego does this. Ego turns everything into a comparison between your self-image and everyone else. Ego always brings out the worst in you. Whether the worst in you is your sense of superiority or your sense of inferiority, ego is responsible for your jealousy, envy, pride, disdain, scorn, and shame.

Ego is a fundamental reason why many people feel so stressed-out much of the time. If you believe your ego, life is an endless competition. Winners succeed. Losers fail. People love winners and they boo the losers. And then, as soon as the winners are built up, the wrecking crew goes to work to tear them down.

Ego will urge you to do all kinds of things to make you look better than others. Ego will run you into the ground to protect its fragile self-image. It's a tough life in a tough world when life is about constant competition to be the best and fear of rejection and ridicule if you don't measure up.

If your sense of who you are is based on *what you think that other people think about you,* you'll live a life defined by too much and too little. Consider how well it turned out for the Evil Queen. She was forced to wear red-hot iron shoes and "dance" until she dropped dead.

A life lived by measuring yourself with others is exhausting, joyless, and relentlessly hard. In other words, it's a guaranteed recipe for feeling stressed-out.

PERMISSION TO SUCCEED

In his book, *Permission to Succeed*, Noah St. John refers to the role of a mirror in determining your sense of yourself. St. John's mirror is not a reflective object on the wall. Rather, it's a metaphor for how you see yourself in other people's opinions of you:

> One of the great ironies of human life is that we can never see ourselves as we truly are but only as we are reflected through the eyes of others.[25]

He contrasts the Negative Reflection and Loving Mirrors:

> The Negative Reflection is simply that part of us that doesn't believe anything good about us and only believes the worst.[26]
>
> ...
>
> What is a Loving Mirror? Simply a person who can love you unconditionally.[27]

The title of St. John's book is his premise: you need *permission* to succeed. This metaphorical mirroring process is still about your ego defining your perception of your self-image. Both *Negative Reflections* and *Loving Mirrors* locate your perception of your self-image in the opinions of others. What you think about yourself depends on feedback from others.

COMPARING YOURSELF TO OTHERS

We live in a society that relentlessly compares and measures people. Most of us didn't learn how to value our own talents and how to develop them. Rather, we learned to measure ourselves in comparison to others, based on the opinions of other people.

We live in an extraordinarily unkind era. Some people judge others relentlessly and cruelly. The internet allows people to write vicious statements and get away with it under the cover of anonymity. Character assassination is a blood sport. Tearing people down is fun. Relentless criticism is the way it is.

Consider what our society does to women in public view. The internet publishes regular features about celebrity clothing choices. Every week, critics proclaim the "worst dressed" and the "best dressed" actors, singers, and entertainers. Almost all of these celebrity images are of women who are displayed as if they were racehorses being paraded before potential buyers. The women pose for the cameras on red carpets, decked out in their high-priced designer outfits. The designers often go to extreme lengths to create distinctive looks for their clients. Some are elegant and some can best be described as bizarre costumes. Nothing is off-limits as the critics comment on clothing, shoes, makeup, jewelry, haircuts, hair color, weight, and age. The comments range from approval to disapproval to ridicule. It's a regular reminder that women are regularly judged for their appearance in ways that rarely apply to men.

For women, appearance really does matter. Fashion magazine articles decree "the latest lip, the best leg, the hottest shoe, the perfect pant." Always singular. It's also an interesting use of language to think of women "wearing" a designer. "Here is Cate Blanchett wearing

Giorgio Armani. Here is Sandra Bullock wearing Alexander McQueen. Here is Emma Watson wearing Valentino."

Another phenomenon has also taken firm root in our culture—the practice of fat shaming. How much stress do you feel about the numbers on your scale? According to the current expectations of society, women cannot be thin enough. Female models are extraordinarily tall and extremely thin, putting even Barbie Doll to shame. We know this from the pronouncements of obese men who sit in front of TV cameras and ridicule gorgeous celebrities as "too fat" if they're not rail thin.

Meanwhile, little girls learn early that being pretty matters more than anything else. Little girls' clothing is designed to be sexy with short shorts and mini bras for little girls. Beauty pageants highlight little girls in tiaras and makeup. Eight year olds worry about whether their "butts are too big." Meanwhile, pink aisles of toy stores include makeup kits, princess dresses, and other "toys" teaching girls that being pretty is more important than being smart. If this isn't enough, girl's clothing often comes with explicit slogans such as "I'm too pretty to do homework, so my brother has to do it for me" or "I'm too pretty to do math."[28]

SELF-IMAGE AND YOUR BOUNDARIES

Your self-image can even set the boundaries of your accomplishments. What *don't* you do because of your appearance? Does your mirror tell you that you're too old, too fat, too unattractive to be taken seriously? Does your image in the mirror tell you that you don't look good enough to do something, so you don't try? How often do you pass up opportunities because your mirror tells you that you don't look good enough? Where *don't* you go because you don't have the right clothes, the right haircut, the right car? Your perception of your appearance can be a formidable obstacle to your willingness to dream, to aspire, and to go out into the world.

Why do you think that your appearance matters so much? You think so because the world we live in has become heavily fixated on appearance, especially for women. An axiom that many American women have taken to heart is the belief that going gray is unacceptable. I have heard success gurus warn that no woman with gray hair can succeed.

I once went to a funeral in a large church in San Francisco. The church was filled with attendees. Most were older couples. From my vantage point about two-thirds of the way back, I observed that the majority of couples attending the service were gray haired men and blond women. This pairing happens often in advertising. A gray haired man and a blond woman look radiantly happy in ads for vacations, golfing, cars, houses, and other symbols of the good life. However, when the advertising is directly addressed to older people for health-related issues, older married couples are often pictured as gray haired men and gray haired women. White haired women appear in ads for scooters, security systems, and assisted living.

Meanwhile, men have their own bad hair days if they have the audacity to go bald. Then the success gurus advise a man to shave his whole head rather than go through life with a bald patch.

These bad hair realities of gray and balding hair are just two examples of contemporary bad hair problems. Among other hair taboos, bad hair includes "ethnic hair" and "mousy hair" and hair that is "too straight" or "too curly." Whatever you identify as your own bad hair problem, what you think about your hair can affect what you think about yourself.

SELF-TALK

Nothing has more power to change your life than monitoring your self-talk.

John Lembo claims:

> Every waking moment we talk to ourselves about the things we experience. Our self-talk, the thoughts we communicate to ourselves, in turn control the way we feel and act.

Ponder the implications of the claim that your self-talk controls the way you feel and act. What exactly are you saying to yourself every waking moment? What's the running conversation you have within yourself about yourself? What do you say about yourself when you look in the mirror? Are you encouraging yourself or are you constantly criticizing yourself?

Lembo's words raise a significant question. Who's doing the talking in your self-talk? If it's your ego-mind, there's no off switch. Your ego-mind will tell you every step of the way whether or not you measure up. If your self-talk is relentless and repetitive criticism and commentary about your faults and failures, you'll always feel bad about yourself. The solution is to practice self-talk that is relentlessly encouraging and uplifting. Whoever you are, and whatever the world thinks of you, you can't change how the world judges you. However, you can change what you say about yourself.

Also consider how other people's opinions of you affect your sense of yourself. Do you have people in your life whose words are relentlessly unkind? Some of us grew up in families where no one has a good word to say about anyone else. This kind of toxic environment can easily foster relentless negative self-talk.

Imagine yourself as a baseball player. When you're the batter and you step up to the plate, what do you hear from your thoughts? Are your thoughts avid fans cheering you on, encouraging your efforts? Are they rooting for you to hit the ball out of the park? Or are your thoughts created by the fans of the opposing team? Are they calling out, "no hitter," yelling out obscenities, criticizing your every move? Which voices are louder? Is anyone rooting for you? Or do you do you take the fans of the opposing team with you every where you go?

Lifelong habits can be tough to overcome, but any habit can be broken with awareness, intention, and commitment. If your inner commentary consists of an endless stream of negative self-talk, it's worth as much effort as it takes to overcome this particular habit. Although you can't change what others say about you, you don't have to follow their example. You can change the way you talk about yourself.

~

QUESTIONS TO THINK ABOUT

1. How much stress in your life is directly related to your self-image?

2. Who do you see when you look into the mirror? Are you satisfied with what you see? Or do you look in the mirror and see only flaws?

3. Do you believe that life is an endless competition?

4. How do other people's opinions of you affect your sense of yourself?

5. Do you need permission from other people to succeed?

6. How does your self-image set the boundaries of your accomplishments? What do you do or not do because of your appearance?

7. What is your self-talk?

8. Who's doing the talking in your self-talk?

9. Does your inner commentary consist of an endless stream of negative self-talk or does it encourage you?

10. What do you hear from your thoughts? Are your thoughts avid fans cheering you on, encouraging your efforts, or are they tearing you down?

Chapter 12

Thinking About
Your Self-Esteem

We all know that self-esteem comes from what you
think of you, not what other people think of you.

Gloria Gaynor

STRESS AND SELF-ESTEEM

How is self-esteem different from self-image? Self-image is about
your ego. Self-image is about your perception of what you look like
in comparison to other people. In contrast, self-esteem is about your
perception of your worth. Ego cannot produce genuine self-esteem
because ego always measures itself in terms of better than or worse
than someone else. In contrast, self-esteem gets out of the
comparison trap. Self-esteem is a high opinion of yourself as yourself
without comparing yourself to other people.

How can you experience self-esteem that doesn't depend on the
opinions of others? Gloria Gaynor's words identify the essential
source of self-esteem: "We all know that self-esteem comes from
what you think of you, not what other people think of you." This
distinction is the difference between living a stressed-out life based
on *what you think other people think about you*, and living a peaceful life
based on your perception of your worth as yourself.

- Self-esteem derives from deep respect and love for who you are at this moment.
- Self-esteem values you more than your accomplishments.
- Self-esteem acknowledges both your strengths and your weaknesses.
- Self-esteem encourages your dreams.
- Self-esteem congratulates you for your accomplishments.

Your self-esteem reveals what you believe about yourself and the value you place on your self. It can't come from any place or anyone outside of you. No matter what anyone else says about you—whether positive or negative—your self-esteem derives from what you believe about yourself. Self-esteem can't be borrowed, it can't be imposed on you, and it can't be taken away from you.

For many people, developing authentic self-esteem means undoing acquired negative beliefs. Many negative beliefs originated in childhood. Small children are sponges who absorb what they hear as truth. If you grow up hearing affirming and encouraging words about yourself, you're very likely to believe that you're capable of doing great things. In contrast, if you grow up hearing only negative comments about you, you'll need to work harder to develop an authentic self-esteem.

How do you undo a lifetime of negative beliefs about yourself? How do you develop authentic self-esteem when your self-image persuades you that you're not capable of handling life's stressors calmly and peacefully? Where do you begin when you're in a life situation that is currently chaotic—perhaps even dangerous—and filled with stressors?

Noah St. John's mirroring process in *Permission to Succeed* can be a life-transforming place to start, but it can't take you all the way to self-esteem because it's based on other people's opinions of you. Creating self-esteem is an inside job.

LANGUAGE AND SELF-ESTEEM

Consider these words attributed to Eleanor Roosevelt:

> No one can make you feel inferior without your consent.

The story behind these words is that the Secretary of Labor in the Roosevelt administration was invited to give a speech at the University of California in Berkeley on the Charter Day of the school. The customary host of the event was unhappy because she thought that the chosen speaker should not have been a political figure. She refused to serve as the host and several newspaper commentators viewed her action as a rebuff and an insult:

> Eleanor Roosevelt was asked at a White House press conference whether the Secretary had been snubbed, and her response was widely disseminated in newspapers. "A snub" defined the first lady, "is the effort of a person who feels superior to make someone else feel inferior. To do so, he has to find someone who can be made to feel inferior." She made clear she didn't think the labor secretary fell within the category of the "snubable."[29]

Whether or not Eleanor Roosevelt herself reformulated these words to become "no one can make you feel inferior without your consent," these words have been attributed to her ever since.

If you're frequently on the receiving end of putdowns, you can write down Eleanor Roosevelt's words and carry them with you. You can post them in a place where you can see them every day. You can ponder carefully what she is saying here and how these words can help when someone says something cruel, demeaning, or highly critical of you. As part of this process, you can observe how you react to negative comments about you. Are you consenting to feel inferior by getting upset over what someone says about you?

You can apply the same perspective to what you say about yourself. You don't have to join the chorus of people criticizing you. If you find yourself comparing yourself to other people, you can remind yourself that life isn't a comparison game. Life is a time to discover your own talents and your own dreams and work to achieve them. Spending time comparing yourself to others doesn't benefit you unless you use other people as inspirations and role models to follow.

SELF-HELP TO BUILD SELF-ESTEEM

One way to build self-esteem is by telling the truth to yourself. Much self-help work promotes affirmations as a way to create success in your life. You declare that you already are, already have, or already do, what you aspire to be, have, or do. Does reciting such affirmations help you develop self-esteem?

Consider what Jim Rohn said about affirmations and truth:

> There is nothing wrong with affirmations, provided what you are affirming is the truth. If you are broke, for example, the best thing to affirm is, "I'm broke."

Although Jim Rohn's words contradict what many self-help teachers tell you about affirmations, these words reveal an essential characteristic of self-esteem: you tell yourself the truth about yourself. You aren't trying to persuade yourself that you're rich when your bank account is down to $1.97. Anyone who has ever heard of affirmations has heard that the subconscious mind doesn't know the difference between reality and your affirmations. This might be true for your subconscious mind, but your conscious mind knows all too well when you're not telling the truth.

What kind of self-esteem can you develop when you don't even tell yourself the truth about your current reality? You'll have a hard time building your own self-esteem if you know that you're lying to yourself. If the truth is that you're broke and you believe that you can be financially successful, it's more empowering to tell that truth than to pretend that you already have everything you want.

CONCENTRATE ON POSSIBILITIES

Denis Waitley claims that:

> Establishing true self-esteem means concentrating on successes and forgetting about the failures and the negatives in your life.

The wisdom behind these words is that you can't have a high estimation of yourself if you spend most of your time analyzing your faults and failures.

One of the great pitfalls of much psychotherapeutic work is that it concentrates on problems rather than on possibilities. Sigmund Freud advocated a self-analysis process to find what was wrong. Freudian psychoanalysis often required years and years of analysis of earlier stages of life. The result of all of this psychoanalysis of the past often produced relentlessly self-critical people who were unable to accomplish much of anything.

In contrast, focusing on where you are in the present and what you aspire to create in the future liberates you. Rather than endlessly analyzing what went wrong in your past, you focus on what you can become. You focus on what you want to create rather than on trying to get rid of your problems. This is the orientation of creator rather than a problem-solver. The more time you spend analyzing your past, the less time and energy you have to focus on what you choose to create.

POSITIVE LANGUAGE AND SELF-ESTEEM

Language can make you or break you. It can lift you up or tear you down. It can liberate you or it can incapacitate you. The world is full of people who have no positive words for anyone. They're always complaining, always finding fault. If you're on the receiving end of such language, you don't have to own it and you don't have to make such negative language your own. You can't develop self-esteem with continual assaults of negative language about yourself. You can choose to think differently and speak differently.

The real power in language is that it defines. Be careful of the words you use to define yourself. Put aside the magnifying glass that looks for your faults. Endless, relentless, self-criticism can't create self-esteem. Rather, focus on what's best in you and the best you can imagine yourself becoming. Above all, tell yourself the truth and be kind to yourself. Positive, truthful language about yourself builds authentic self-esteem.

SELF-ESTEEM AND JUDGMENT

You also can't build authentic self-esteem by judging yourself in comparison to others. Judgments separate. Judgments decide who's better and who's worse, who's worthy and who's unworthy, who's capable and who's incapable.

Although comparing yourself to other people can build up your ego self-image, you can't build authentic self-esteem by judging yourself in relationship to other people. If you encounter someone who is better than you in some way, your ego-created perception of yourself becomes a balloon that is poked with a sharp knife. If your attempt to build self-esteem is built on such judgments, your opinion of yourself rests on a fragile and tenuous foundation.

In contrast, authentic self-esteem comes from a deep appreciation of yourself. Self-esteem concerns your self-assessment, your intentions, your values, and your choices. You build your self-esteem when you uphold your own values with integrity. You can't develop authentic self-esteem by asking permission or by comparing yourself to others. You can only develop self-esteem by learning to value yourself.

INTENTION FOR OTHERS

One of the most powerful forces you can use in your life is your intention. If you intend the best for others, including genuinely hoping that they succeed in their goals, you'll open up a powerful capacity in yourself to get beyond jealousy and resentment of someone else's success.

Anytime you harbor resentment against someone else's success, you're limiting your own potential. You're trapped in your ego-mind, where you're always comparing yourself to someone else, either favorably or unfavorably. You'll be free of that burden when you adopt a different perspective toward others. Someone else's success doesn't diminish you, unless you allow it by comparing yourself negatively to that person. You can move beyond comparison to a mindset of intending the best for others. When you are genuinely glad for their successes, you expand your own capacity for success.

High self-esteem reflects the belief that the world has room for you and others to succeed. High self-esteem allows others to use their talents as you develop yours. You can admire and be inspired by other people and use their lives as examples for you to develop your own skills and fulfill your dreams. However, when you compare yourself to others as better than or worse than, your ego-mind blocks your capacity to fulfill your own dreams. Your ego-mind lies as it generates stress in your life. In an ego-driven world, competition is the name of the game. Comparison warns you that the success of someone else jeopardizes your success.

YOUR UNIQUE LIFE

How can you stop stressing yourself by comparing yourself and your talents to other people? You do it by recognizing and accepting that your life is unique. No one on Earth is exactly like you. No one who has ever lived or ever will live was or will be exactly like you. Self-esteem acknowledges that you have your own unique talents and gifts and insights to bring to the world.

~

?DO YOU HAVE HIGH SELF-ESTEEM?

1. What is your perception of your worth?
2. What negative beliefs about yourself can you replace with self-esteem?
3. Are you consenting to feel inferior by getting upset over what someone says about you?
4. Do you tell the truth to yourself?
5. Do you concentrate on your successes or your failures?
6. How do you focus on creating the life you want rather than trying to fix your problems?
7. Do you intend the best for others?
8. Do you recognize and accept that your life is unique?

Chapter 13

Thinking About
Your Self-Trust

Self-trust is often overlooked yet it is the most
powerful virtue we have. In order to succeed in
anything we must possess this ability. Otherwise we
are living through someone else.

Suzanne Jones

STRESS AND SELF-TRUST

Self-image is your ego perception of yourself in comparison to other
people. Self-esteem is your high opinion of your own value without
comparing yourself to other people. A third type of perception about
yourself is self-trust. Trust is a confident belief in someone's
character, reliability, ability, and truthfulness. Self-trust is your own
confidence in your own character, reliability, ability, and
truthfulness. The connection between stress and self-trust concerns
how much confidence you have in your own trustworthiness to
respond to stressors in your life.

Two types of stressors test your trust in yourself. The first type of
stressor concerns external threats and potential catastrophes. A
Category 5 hurricane heads your way, or a powerful earthquake jolts
your house so badly that you're afraid it's going to fall down on top of
you, or an uncontrolled fire races toward your home. You can also

feel stressed-out if you live with a dangerous, unpredictably violent person, or live in a hostile environment. Such stressors require more than a change of attitude or mindset.

The second type of stressor concerns responsibilities in your daily life, such as earning an income, doing housework and home maintenance, going to work, paying bills, buying food, fixing meals, doing laundry, taking care of children, driving on busy roads. If you feel stressed-out most of the time by these daily stressors, feeling stressed-out has become a way of life.

If you find yourself feeling stressed-out much of the time, ask yourself if your stress is a vote of no confidence in yourself. Do you trust that you can take care of yourself and those who depend on you? Do you trust that you can earn or create the money necessary to pay for what you want and need? Do you trust your character to be reliable, to tell the truth, to do the right thing? Do you have confidence that you can do whatever you need to do in the face of any stressor?

This list is only the beginning. You can list your own stressors. What or who demands more, expects more, needs more than you feel able to give? Stressed-out is a sense of helplessness, the sense of being squeezed and unable to do anything about it. Underneath it all, feeling stressed-out as a way of life demonstrates a fundamental lack of trust in your capacity to do what needs to be done.

Lack of self-trust plays the mantra in your head:

- I can't do this.
- I'm not smart enough.
- I don't know enough.
- I don't trust myself and my decisions.

The antidote to this kind of debilitating stress is self-trust. When you trust yourself, you trust you can deal with anything that comes your way. You have confidence in your abilities to make good choices and to carry out your plans. You have confidence that you'll be resourceful enough to solve whatever problems show up in your life. Self-trust develops when you believe in your own power, abilities, and capacities.

Consider the words of Suzanne Jones:

> Self-trust is often overlooked yet it is the most powerful virtue we have. In order to succeed in anything we must possess this ability. Otherwise we are living through someone else.

Her second sentence is particularly insightful. She claims that if you don't trust yourself, you'll be living your life through someone else. Living through someone else is when you allow someone else to make your decisions for you, or even worse, when you're bullied into doing what you don't want to do, or prevented from doing what you do want to do. Self-trust grows when you believe that you have the capacity to make your own decisions and succeed at what you decide to do.

The most successful people in the world trust their own dreams and abilities. In the face of opposition or ridicule, they make their own choices and have confidence in their own capacity to do what needs to be done to accomplish their intentions.

THE SELF-TRUST OF MALALA YOUSAFZAI

Albert Einstein said this after the assassination of Mahatma Gandhi:

> Generations to come will scarce believe that such a one as this ever in flesh and blood walked upon this earth.

This generation is already experiencing a similar reaction to a Pakistani girl named Malala Yousafzai. She is the youngest person ever to receive a Nobel Prize. Her desire to be educated, and her conviction that every child everywhere deserves the right to be educated, led to an attempted assassination attempt against her by the Taliban.

Before the assassination attempt, she wrote about what she would say to the Taliban if they came to kill her:

> I think of it often and imagine the scene clearly. Even if they come to kill me, I will tell them what they are trying to do is wrong, that education is our basic right.

After the Taliban's unsuccessful assassination attempt, she said this:

> The terrorists thought they would change my aims and stop my ambitions, but nothing changed in my life except this: weakness, fear and hopelessness died. Strength, power and courage was born ... I am not against anyone, neither am I here to speak in terms of personal revenge against the Taliban or any other terrorist group. I'm here to speak up

for the right of education for every child. I want education for the sons and daughters of the Taliban and all terrorists and extremists.[30]

Both of these statements demonstrate that her courage and convictions are built on an extraordinary sense of self-trust. She trusts in the rightness of her belief that education for all children everywhere is a basic right and she trusts in her own strength, power, and courage to be an advocate.

LEARNING TO TRUST YOURSELF

One of the realities of our society is that few of us are taught to trust ourselves. In this case, Malala Yousafzai had an enormous advantage. She received much of her education from her father. He owned a chain of schools and was committed to education for all children. He recognized her extraordinary talents and encouraged her political activism. His commitment to education and his trust in his daughter were strong foundations for building Malala's self-trust. Malala also acknowledges the strong support of her mother:

And then there's another person we don't mention all the time: my mother. My mother always encourages us to continue this campaign. She believes that what we are doing is the truth and we should never be afraid of telling the truth.[31]

How many of us received such support from our parents? Did you? Or were you taught to fulfill the plans of others? Were you taught how to discover your own talents, gifts, and callings? Or were your desires, hopes, and dreams demeaned and suppressed by the people closest to you?

How does this relate to stress? If you were taught to be obedient to the will of others, you might not recognize the connection between your stress and your inner urgings. Stress results when you spend your life doing what doesn't resonate with your desires and talents. It's very stressful to have a dream and be told that you must give up your dreams to fulfill someone else's demands for your life. When this happens, you're living through someone else.

The remedy for this kind of stress is to learn to trust yourself and your own desires for your life. When you're willing to trust your own knowing, you'll discover what you feel compelled to do, what you'd love to do, what kind of work would engage your mind, what would excite your creative desires.

How do you learn to trust yourself when you've lived a lifetime learning how to follow the rules, color within the lines, and do what other people tell you to do? Would the world ever have heard of Malala Yousafzai if her father had built a chain of schools for boys only and insisted that girls should not be educated? Would Malala speak with such conviction and demonstrate such courage if she did not have this kind of support from her parents?

Self-trust is easier to build when the significant people in your life trust you first. What do you do if you never experienced this kind of trust from anyone in your life? Whatever else you do, awareness of the words you use is critical to learning to trust yourself. What do you say to yourself? Is your language filled with statements about what you can't do, don't know how to do, are unable to do? Or is your language filled with the words expressing your own belief that you can trust yourself to do what you need to do, learn what you need to learn, and trust that you can find the help you need?

Learning to trust yourself is an essential element in creating the kind of life you desire to live. Golda Meir said this about self-trust:

> Trust yourself. Create the kind of self that you will be happy to live with all your life. Make the most of yourself by fanning the tiny, inner sparks of possibility into flames of achievement.

YOUR HIDDEN POTENTIAL

You can build self-trust by reminding yourself that human beings have extraordinary capacities in times of crisis. People do heroic acts to save others. You'll see stories about how a mother lifts a car to get it off her child. She couldn't have imagined doing such a thing because women don't have that kind of strength—except that she did when her child's life was at stake. Soldiers do impossibly courageous acts to accomplish their missions and save the lives of other soldiers. How about the two sisters who lifted a tractor off their father to save his life? The world is full of stories of ordinary people doing extraordinary acts in times of crisis.[32]

You don't have to be in a crisis situation to tap into your abilities to do more than you imagine yourself doing. When you think about your life, do you remember times when you got something you wanted, because you wanted it and did everything you could do to get it? Think about those times. Remember your own resilience. Such memories can remind you that you have more potential than you realize.

Your trust in your ability to deal with challenges correlates with your level of stress. If you trust yourself, you aren't going to be engulfed with stressed-out feelings. Going through life feeling stressed-out indicates that you don't trust yourself to be able to do what you need to do.

The renowned baby doctor, Dr. Benjamin Spock, said:

Trust yourself, you know more than you think you do.

It's so easy to overlook your skills—the skills that you had to work hard to master. You can learn to trust yourself to handle some new task if you acknowledge how much you already know and what you have already done.

You can make an inventory of what you know to do. Write down all of the tasks you do on a daily basis without thinking about them. You can start with basic skills, such as walking, feeding yourself, tying your shoes. At one time, you didn't know how to do any of these actions. Now you can. How about reading? Writing? Being able to add and subtract? Drive a car? Do you remember being nervous when you learned to drive? You had to learn how to steer, how to back up, how to turn corners, how to make good decisions on the road. It's worth making your list as long as possible to remind yourself that you didn't arrive on Earth knowing how to do any of these actions. Acknowledge that your own life history demonstrates that you can learn whatever new skills you need.

Even more significantly, ask yourself if you trust your ability to walk, tie, your shoes, feed yourself? Do you trust yourself to read and write, to add and subtract, to drive a car? Do you trust yourself to do everything you put on your list? If you look at all that you trust yourself to do on a daily basis, you'll discover that you already have a great reservoir of self-trust.

SELF-TRUST AND COMMUNICATION

Self-trust is essential for effective communication. If you trust yourself, you'll communicate clearly about what you observe, what you know, what you intend, and what you desire. If you're communicating with someone you trust, you can tell the truth, state your honest opinions, and offer creative solutions.

What happens when lack of trust shapes your communication? What if you don't trust the communication you get from someone else? What if you don't dare to speak your truth? If these factors are involved, your communication will be stressful. You might feel that you're walking on eggshells. You have to be careful not to offend to avoid triggering an outburst of anger or some scathing criticism.

If you don't trust the person giving you the information, you'll be wary about what you say and what you hear. Without shared trust, communication becomes a stressful interaction that leads only to more distrust.

TRUST AND RELATIONSHIPS

Mutual trust is the glue that holds relationships together. Mutual trust creates happiness, joy, friendship, and love. Mutual trust also creates successful business ventures, partnerships, and workplaces. You don't worry about betrayals, about lies, about deceptions. You don't wonder what's hidden. You don't feel the need to hide, sidestep, or withhold what you know.

A relationship without trust is like dancing wearing armor. It's hard to move and utterly lacking in grace. A relationship without trust involves sleights of hand, deceptions, and misdirections. Distrust poisons relationships. Marriages break up when trust dies. Friendships die. Partnerships end.

How does lack of trust relate to stress? Unless you're a psychopath or sociopath who lies habitually without remorse, lying is stressful. It's also stressful to realize that someone is lying to you. Lying can destroy the longest lasting relationships.

Your goal is to avoid being either naïve or cynical. Consider the words of Eric Hoffer:

> Someone who thinks the world is always cheating him is right. He is missing that wonderful feeling of trust in someone or something.

If you go through life untrusting of yourself and others, you're blinding yourself to what is best in yourself and others. Your lack of trust in yourself and others results in a stressful life.

SELF-TRUST AND INTUITION

A valuable aspect of self-trust is intuition. Stephen King observed:

> The trust of the innocent is the liar's most useful tool.

Psychopaths and sociopaths exist. If you're paying attention to your intuitions, you'll get warnings about people. You'll begin to recognize the difference between your intuitions and ordinary thoughts. You might already be aware that you're intuitive. Or you might not be aware that each of us has capacities that can't be explained by ordinary thinking. You might have a sudden insight, thought, or perception about something. You might know something without being able to say how you know it. You have no proof, no evidence, and yet you know. Circumstances soon verify your perception. If you've never had such an experience, this kind of intuition might seem farfetched. If you have, you already know the value of trusting your intuition.

Gisele Bündchen asserts:

> The more you trust your intuition, the more empowered you become, the stronger you become, and the happier you become.

If you have doubts about people, trust your doubts. You'll discover that you can be open and honest with most people. Others are not trustworthy. If you trust your insights, you'll recognize those you can trust and those you can't.

SELF-TRUST AND MONEY

How does money relate to self-trust? In her best-selling book, Marsha Sinetar wrote:

> Do what you love, the money will follow.[33]

Some dispute this premise. They claim that you need to do what the marketplace demands. If you want to make money, follow Zig Ziglar's adage:

> Give people what they want and they will give you what you want.

Can you trust that if you do what you love, you'll make enough money to support yourself? Once again, it comes down to self-trust. Can you trust yourself to make your own life decisions? Can you trust that your desires can lead you to financial success? The correct answer is that no one knows. You don't know. And the people who tell you that it's impractical to follow your dreams don't know either.

Trust in yourself gives you the freedom to do what you love and learn what you need. Trust allows you to believe that you have the ability if you commit to learning the essential skills through disciplined practice.

I don't remember who said it, or his exact words, but I do remember essence of the words of a renowned classical pianist. After a concert, a woman proclaimed to him: "I would love to play the piano the way you do." He replied: "No, you don't. If you did, you would practice eight hours a day, seven days a week the way I do."

This is what it comes down to. Intuition and desire do not imbue you with magical skills. They only point you in the direction. If you claim that you would love to do something, are you willing to commit the time and effort to do it? Can you trust yourself that you will follow through?

The great hockey player Wayne Gretzky spoke words of enduring wisdom when he said:

You miss one hundred percent of the shots you don't take.

You can't know ahead of time if following your dreams will bring you wealth or fame or success or happiness. The only thing that you can know for certain is that you can't fulfill your dreams if you don't trust yourself enough to take your shots.

~

QUESTIONS TO THINK ABOUT

1. Do you trust yourself?

2. Do you have confidence in your own character, reliability, ability, and truthfulness?

3. Are you living through someone else?

4. Were your desires, hopes, and dreams demeaned and suppressed by the people closest to you?

5. Does your language express your own belief that you can trust yourself to do what you need to do, learn what you need to learn, and trust that you can find the help you need?

6. When did you get something you wanted, because you wanted it and did everything you could do to get it?

7. Do you trust your intuition?

8. Do you trust yourself to make your own life decisions?

PART V

THINKING ABOUT
RE-CREATING YOUR SELF

Chapter 14

Thinking About Re-Creating Your Self

Life isn't about finding yourself. Life is about creating yourself.

George Bernard Shaw

STRESS AND LIFE CHANGE

The idea of changing your life is pervasive in our contemporary world. Books, articles, training programs, DVDs, CDs, blog posts, videos, and every other medium you can imagine claim that you can change your life if you follow their methods. Why is this phrase so prevalent? The phrase identifies a universal desire in human beings to solve the inevitable problems of human life.

The root meaning of the word *change* is to "substitute one for another." A desire to change your life means that you want to exchange something in your life for something else. In this case, the "something" is stress. You feel stressed-out and you don't want to feel that way. Your desire to change your life means that you want to exchange your stressed-out feelings for something else. How do you make this kind of change in your life?

Consider these three approaches as solutions to the problem of living your life feeling stressed-out:

- Fixing your self
- Discovering your True Self
- Creating your self

FIXING YOUR SELF

Much self-help work builds on two assumptions. The first is overt. The second is covert. The first assumption asserts that you can change your life by fixing how you deal with some problem in your life. The second assumption is less obvious, but it's the assumption that lies beneath so much of what western cultures believe about human life.

The first assumption describes traditional psychotherapy. How you deal with stress is a problem to be fixed. Consider this definition by the National Institute of Mental Health:

> *Psychotherapy*, or "talk therapy", is a way to treat people with a mental disorder by helping them understand their illness. It teaches people strategies and gives them tools to deal with stress and unhealthy thoughts and behaviors.[34]

Ponder carefully what this definition claims about you and stress. It identifies your experience of stress as a mental disorder. It also claims that you can "deal with stress" if you have the right strategies and tools.

This psychotherapeutic approach to stress is familiar ground. Whatever the benefit of this approach to understand how you think about your life and how you can deal with stress in your life, the primary assumptions of the model are:

- Stress exists as an entity apart from you.
- Something in you needs to be fixed.

A more liberating approach begins by thinking differently about stress and your self.

DISCOVERING YOUR TRUE SELF

Some of the wisest words in human history were written on the ancient Temple of Apollo at Delphi:

Know yourself.

The words *Know Yourself* can also define the second prevalent assumption about stress in your life. This covert assumption shapes much of what we believe about who we are.

Western culture is deeply rooted in Greek philosophical ideas going back to Plato's belief that anything that exists in the material world takes its *material Form* from a *non-material Form* in the *Ideal plane*. The non-material Form is unchangeable. If you apply this assumption to yourself, the *Real You* exists as a changeless non-material Form in the Ideal plane. This Platonic influence leads to the dominating assumption of much non-therapeutic self-help work:

Your *True Self* is hidden within you.

Based on this assumption, changing your life means discovering your *True Self*. (The capitalization emphasizes the claim that this hidden you is the *Real You*.) This claim means that your stress problems are not signs of mental disorder but they do involve a kind of amnesia or mistaken identity. The problems of your life—including your stress experiences—demonstrate that you don't know your True Self. You know only your False Self that obscures your True Self from you. Based on this assumption, self-help becomes a quest, a journey, an exploration, an excavation, as you seek to discover your True Self hidden away within you.

A frequently cited metaphor for this kind of self-help work concerns Michelangelo's statue of David:

> When they asked Michelangelo how he made his statue of David he is reported to have said, "It is easy. You just chip away the stone that doesn't look like David."[35]

Although it's highly unlikely that Michelangelo ever made such a statement, these words attributed to him have taken on a life of their own as a defining metaphor for discovering your True Self: you find your True Self by chipping away your False Self.

For example, think about these words by James Ryan in his excellent book, *Screenwriting from the Heart*. He makes the case that characters do not *change* in stories. Instead they *discover* hidden parts of themselves:

> What happens in any good story is not that characters change, but rather, their circumstances have forced them to take a new tack, and parts of their character that were previously dormant, suddenly open up and are revealed.[36]

The claim that parts of your character are dormant within you assumes that your True Self exists as a distinct entity within you. Although I have cited this particular quotation elsewhere, I now consider the idea that "parts of their character that were previously dormant, suddenly open up and are revealed" demonstrates the primary fallacy of efforts to "discover your True Self." This quest for your True Self—your Authentic Self—means that life is a quest for hidden treasure as you seek to find your perfect, whole, stress-free True Self within you.[37]

CREATING YOUR SELF

The third approach to solving the problem of unwanted stress in your life goes beyond psychotherapeutic methods to fix yourself or efforts to find your hidden True Self. The third approach focuses on *creating your self*. George Bernard Shaw defines the essential difference between efforts to discover your True Self and your potential to create your self:

> Life isn't about finding yourself. Life is about creating yourself.

The essential difference between *finding* and *creating* concerns existence. It's the difference between *what is* and *what you cause to be*. When you *discover,* you can find only what now exists. In contrast, *creating* brings something into existence.

The meaning of creating also demonstrates the fundamental difference between problem solving and creating. Problem solving makes something you don't want go away. Creating causes something you do want to exist.

Rather than fixing yourself or finding yourself, creating your self is a process to create a new life. You don't limit yourself to attempts to solve the problems of your current life. You also don't spend time trying to find your ostensibly hidden True Self. Rather you create a new life with a new orientation.

When you take on the identity of a creator rather than a problem to be solved or a seeker after your hidden True Self, you give yourself access to the realm of almost unlimited possibilities. You begin by imagining what you would like to become and then you develop a process to fulfill that vision. A decision to create a new life to fulfill your dreams rather than treating your life as a problem to be solved—with you as the primary problem—is simultaneously thrilling and challenging.

CONSTANT CHANGE

A quest to discover your hidden True Self ignores the fundamental reality of life on Earth. Everything on Earth—including you—exists in a constant state of change.

Look again at the words of James Ryan:

> What happens in any good story is not that characters change, but rather, their circumstances have forced them to take a new tack, and parts of their character that were previously dormant, suddenly open up and are revealed.

Now look at his words from the following page:

> A character is a dynamic entity—the possibilities are nearly endless. There is much about characters an author will not

know until the characters are forced by circumstances and external pressures to express parts of themselves that are dormant. [37]

In this paragraph, Ryan identifies a character as a "dynamic entity." He follows this with a sentence that refers to "parts of themselves that are dormant." The mixing of "dynamic entity" and "dormant" parts confounds the matter. *Dynamic* is derived from Greek and means "power." Dynamic refers to power in continuous active, changing, and energetic motion. *Dormant* is derived from Latin and means "asleep." Dormant means being asleep and inactive.

The significant word is "possibilities." It's derived from the Latin *potentia*, which means "power, might, force." A possibility is potential power that something might exist, happen, or be true.

If the language about "dormant parts" is changed in both quotations, the words express the reality of all living beings as well as all components of the natural world: all living beings evolve. *Evolve* derives from *evolvere*, which means to "roll out." To evolve is to change slowly over time. Earth itself is in a constant process of evolution. Continents move. Oceans open and close. Mountains grow and shrink. You evolve too. You're constantly evolving day-by-day in an environment where change is the only constant. Every day you're different from the day before. No static, perfect Real You hides within you. What does exist within you is the potential to evolve, to develop, and to become.

You have far more possibilities than you either know or use. Changing your life is not about discovering dormant parts of a hidden True Self. Rather it's about discovering that you have almost unlimited potential to create the life you choose to live.

INNER AND OUTER PROCESS

Creating the life you choose is both an inner and an outer process. External changes aren't enough. You can't change your stressed-out life until you think differently about stress in your life. You begin by paying attention to how you think, what you say, and what you do. Life change requires thinking different thoughts, dreaming different dreams, and taking different actions.

Re-creating your life also requires examining and changing your beliefs. Beliefs can be particularly tenacious, especially beliefs that you learned as a child. You learned to believe what you were taught without questioning the validity of what you learned.

Remember that Einstein said:

> The significant problems we face cannot be solved at the same level of thinking we were at when we created them.

A corollary to this statement is that you can't change what you think and believe with the mind that accepted what you learned as accurate and valid.

TRANSFORMATION FROM STRESSED-OUT TO PEACEFUL

Can you change your life from stressed-out to peaceful? You can if you're willing to go through your own unique creation process. The process to turn a stressed-out life into a peaceful life requires determination, commitment, and a vision of what you can become.

You begin with an idea. What do you desire to become? Then you do the necessary inner work to turn your idea into reality. Over time, you become what you dreamed of becoming.

As a model for your creation process, consider the process of metamorphosis that turns a caterpillar into a butterfly. *Metamorphosis* is "transformation"—change in form. The life of a butterfly-to-be begins with the egg. The egg has potential but has not yet taken any sort of recognizable shape. It begins as raw materials that will turn into a living entity. An egg is fragile and needs to be protected. A tiny caterpillar—the *larva*—emerges from the egg. Its task is to eat as much as possible to grow into a larger caterpillar. The next stage is when metamorphosis occurs. The caterpillar creates a silken cocoon and undergoes the process of turning into a butterfly. In this stage, the form of the caterpillar is completely unmade as it becomes a *pupa* (also called a *chrysalis*). The transformation is complete when the pupa becomes a butterfly.

Human beings don't undergo this kind of physical metamorphosis from one form to another. However, you can learn much about transforming your life from these stages in the life cycle of a butterfly.

The egg stage of your own creative transformation process is an idea. Creation begins with a compelling thought. The thought has potential, but has not yet taken any sort of recognizable shape. Both eggs and new ideas are fragile and break easily. Since your nascent idea needs to be protected, you allow it to develop in safety until it's ready to emerge.

In the larva stage of your creative transformation process you feed your caterpillar idea. You give it what it needs to grow, through study, research, and testing. Your caterpillar idea probably won't bear much resemblance to the finished butterfly form of your idea.

Although it isn't beautiful and can't fly, this stage is necessary to build the foundation for your creation.

Early stages in a creative process often don't reveal what is to come. Consider the construction site of a large building. In the beginning, most of the work goes into laying the foundation of the building. A large building project can involve months of trucks coming and going, concrete being poured, and pilings sunk into the ground. None of this will be visible when the building is finished. No one will admire the structure and lines of the pilings, yet without this kind of careful preparation, no building will be strong enough, stable enough, and grounded enough to stand.

In any creative process, much of the essential early work is hidden. No one will know or care how much you worked on it. Creating the life you choose begins with laying the foundation for what you choose to become. Whether or not your idea lives or dies depends on your stamina and how long you're willing to do the underground work.

The next stage is the cocoon stage when you develop your idea. You have built the foundation. Now it's time to build the building. It's time for the caterpillar to turn into a butterfly. Being alone is part of that process. Otherwise you'll get derailed by the advice and opinions of others.

THE SECRET OF SUCCESS

One of the most insightful suggestions I have ever heard about writing was a statement by Ginie Sayles in a Learning Annex writing class in San Francisco. She said, "The secret of success is to keep it secret." She defined her own book-writing process to write a novel in three weeks. It involved working each weekday evening and spending the weekends in intensive, focused work on her project. Her process—as I remember it—involved three factors. The first factor was concentrated time working on her book. The second factor was intense focus in isolation. The third factor was using a story as a template. For her novels, she used a familiar fairy tale as the template for her stories.

Time, isolated focus, and a template. All are essential for turning an egg into a butterfly or idea into a completed creation. The factor that is particularly insightful concerns the idea of isolated focus—the equivalent of the pupal stage when the caterpillar metamorphoses into a butterfly. This is the cocoon stage.

For a specific example of why "the secret of success is keeping it secret" can be the difference between creating what you love and being derailed by the opinions of others, consider this example. I once took a three-month screenwriting class. The class met in San Francisco once a week for three hours. I discovered in the first session that it was an ongoing class. Some of the students had taken the three-month class several times.

We sat at tables arranged in a rectangular shape so that we all faced each other. Students talked about the stories they were writing and asked for feedback. A young man in his early twenties talked about the first scene of the first act of his screenplay. Several people commented and made suggestions about what he needed to fix.

The next week, he again talked about the first scene of the first act of his screenplay. And again, the helpful critics made more comments and suggestions about what he needed to fix.

In the third week, he and I talked briefly before class. In that conversation, I discovered that he had been taking that class for more than a year and had not gotten beyond the first scene of the first act. Every week, the helpful critics tore his idea apart. Each week the young man looked more and more dejected, but he went home and tried to redo the first scene of the first act.

Although I admired his persistence, I began to hope that he would decide to stop taking the class, stay at home, and write a complete first draft of the whole story. He had only a vague idea of his story. How could he write a beginning when he had no idea of the ending? The last thing he needed was "helpful advice and constructive criticism." He needed time alone to turn his egg into a caterpillar and the caterpillar into a butterfly. Caterpillars turn into butterflies in cocoons. They don't re-create themselves in public view.

This story demonstrates the wisdom of Ginie Sayles's aphorism. The secret of success is to keep it secret while you're creating it. Whatever you're creating, the path of wisdom is to keep it secret while it's taking shape. You can ask for feedback later, but let it take shape before you expose it to the world. Both you and your creation need time and space to be alone.

Whatever you desire to create, the steps aren't as linear as the re-creation from egg to butterfly, but the essential truth of the re-creation is the same. Real change takes time. You don't remake your life overnight. The idea might come overnight, but the doing takes longer. Taking apart the old and creating a new life takes time, awareness, and perseverance.

YOUR VISION

What's your vision of the life you desire to create? Your vision might not be clear at first. As you determine what truly matters to you, what you desire to create, what you desire to do, your vision will become clearer. As you begin to develop your vision, be mindful of how you talk about your vision. Often the people who are least supportive of your idea are the people closest to you in your life. Families are often notorious dream-killers. They throw cold water on your dream, tell you that you don't have what it takes to become what you want. Maybe you're very fortunate and the people in your family will support you. Most families aren't sources of inspiration and encouragement. They claim to know you too well.

Friends can also undermine you. You might find that you need new friends. If people aren't willing to change their lives, they're not going to support your efforts to change yours. Inertia and habit are two powerful forces working against you. If you can't find support and encouragement for your vision of what you desire to become from the people in your life, you can find support and encouragement from people who are actively seeking to re-create their own lives.

You change stressed-out into a peaceful life, not by trying to fix what's wrong with you, or by trying to find your hidden True Self. Rather, you become the creator of your own peaceful life. You can't get a road map from anyone else. Your peaceful life journey is yours to create.

~

QUESTIONS TO THINK ABOUT

1. Do you consider yourself a problem to be solved?
2. Do you assume that you have to find your hidden true self to change your life?
3. Do believe you can create a new life for yourself
4. Do you focus on your problems or your possibilities?
5. What do you desire to become?
6. How does the process of metamorphosis that turns a caterpillar into a butterfly provide a model for you to transform your life?
7. Do you need to keep something secret to succeed?
8. What's your vision of the life you desire to create?

Chapter 15

Thinking About
The Language of Creation

Language helps form the limits of our reality.

Dale Spender

LANGUAGE AND STRESS

People who are creators speak a different language than people who feel habitually stressed-out. They might all be speaking English—or some other shared language—but they use different syntax and different words to describe their lives.

Syntax refers to the structure of your sentences. Merriam Webster defines syntax as:

> The way in which words are put together to form phrases, clauses, or sentences.

The most significant syntactical difference between creators and frequently stressed-out people concerns the subjects and direct objects of their sentences. Consider the syntactical function of the word "you" in these sentences:

- Heavy traffic stresses you.
- Your boss stresses you.
- Shopping stresses you.
- Your children stress you.
- Filing taxes stresses you.

Compare the first group of sentences with these sentences:

- You drive calmly in heavy traffic.
- You talk confidently with the boss.
- You enjoy taking care of the children.
- You file the tax return on time with no problems.

Think about what role *you* play in these sentences. In the first group of sentences, *you* is the direct object of the sentence. In the second group, *you* is the subject of the sentence. The direct object *receives* the action of the verb. The subject of the sentence *does* the action of the verb.

If *you* are the subject of the sentence, *you* are the active doer. If *you* are the direct object, the subject of the sentence does something *to you*. For example, if *you* are the subject, *you* hit the baseball. If *you* are the direct object, the baseball hits *you*. If *you* are the subject, *you* bite the dog. If *you* are the direct object, the dog bites *you*.

In the first group of sentences, someone or something other than *you* is the subject of the sentence—traffic, the boss, shopping, children, taxes. *They* are the people or conditions that *cause you* to experience stress. As the direct object, *you* don't have a verb of your own. *You* don't *do* anything, except be stressed by *their* unwanted actions. As the direct object of the sentence, *you* are the baseball that gets hit with the bat, *you* are the victim of a dog bite, and *you* are the hapless victim of people or circumstances who *cause you* to feel stressed-out.

In contrast, the second group of sentences makes *you* the active doer. In these sentences, *you* do the action of the verb. The traffic, the boss, the children, and the tax return are no longer the ones that *cause you* to experience stress. Significantly, the word *stress* is missing in these sentences.

This syntactical difference between the subject and direct object might seem like trivial grammatical nitpicking, but it's a powerful tool to reveal how you live in the world. This distinction turns you from the object of some stressor into the creator of something that you choose to create. If you think about the syntax of subject-verb-direct object in the sentences you speak and the thoughts you think, you can go a long way to change your life from the stressed-out victim of circumstances to creator of the life you choose.

THE VOCABULARY OF CREATORS

In addition to this difference in syntax, creators use a distinctive vocabulary that sets them apart from people who feel habitually stressed-out by other people and life circumstances. Three essential words for creators are: *creation; choice; love.*

The first essential word is *creation.* A creation is something you make. A creator makes something that doesn't currently exist in the world. It's the opposite action to solving a problem. A problem is something you don't want in your world. Problem solving gets rid of something you don't want. Creation brings something into existence that you do want.

The second essential word is *choice*. When you create, you choose to bring something into existence that does not currently exist in your life. A creator has no need for words such as *have to, ought to, must,* or *should.* Rather the language of a creator is the language of choice.

The third essential word is *love*. When you create, you bring something into existence because you would love to have it in your life. Love is not the language you use when you attempt to solve a problem. The defining characteristic of a problem is that you don't want it in your life. The defining characteristic of a creation is that you do want it and you're eager to love it into existence.

WHAT ARE YOUR DREAMS?

When I was in college years ago, a friend told me about her future plans. She said that she wanted to be an artist, but she'd have to wait until after the children were grown to follow her own interests. Even then, her vision for her future astonished me. She was nineteen. She had no children. She was neither married nor engaged. She had no steady boyfriend. Already, she was putting her dream to be an artist on hold until after her future children were grown.

Think about your dreams. What did you imagine doing when you were younger? Did you also preemptively surrender your dreams to the practical realities of being grown-up? Did you give up your dreams of doing great things, of going places, of making a difference in the world?

If life is just about fixing problems, dealing with crises, and repairing what doesn't work, life turns into a rather joyless experience of plodding along, always reacting to what you don't like and don't want. Meanwhile, you tell yourself that you *don't have time* to do the things you'd love to do. Such a life wears you down and breaks your spirit.

STRESSED-OUT BY TOO LITTLE RATHER THAN TOO MUCH

How does this tradeoff of your dreams for adult responsibilities relate to your ongoing experience of stress? Think about Marcus Buckingham's claim:

> Many of us feel stress and get overwhelmed not because we're taking on too much, but because we're taking on too little of what really strengthens us.

Stress is a reaction to a stressor. Something occurs or exists that you don't want. The stressor is a problem to solve, to get rid of this unwanted intruder in your life.

What if you feel stressed-out because you believe that you don't have enough time to do what you'd love to do, to create what you'd love to create? How would your life change if you made room in your life to follow your dreams?

Something inherent in human beings loves to create. Whether you're composing a symphony, creating a garden, building a bookcase, building a business, writing a book, or making a pie, when you create, you're spending your time doing what you love rather than what you don't love.

Imagine how your life would be different if you spent most of your time doing what you love rather than spending your time dealing with what you don't want in your life. The quality of your life depends on where you put your attention. If you spend most of your time reacting to problems, you're missing the empowering experience of doing what you love to do.

You begin by imagining possibilities. Imagination is an essential part of the creative process. Albert Einstein claimed:

Imagination is more important than knowledge.[38]

Imagination allows you to see something in your mind that doesn't exist in the present. The ability to imagine allows you to look beyond your current stress-inducing experiences and imagine a life that isn't ruled by your reactions to outside stressors. What would you change? What you would do? Who you would be? Instead of seeing yourself as the victim of stressors, you can imagine yourself as the creator of your peaceful life. In your vision, you become the visionary, the storyteller, the artist, and the builder of your life.

Creation brings something desirable into your existence. If you go through life as a creator, you see opportunities to make your life better, more interesting, more fun, and more satisfying. Being aware of the distinctions between problem solving and creation can help you turn a life filled with stressed-out reactions into the experience of creating what you want. Ask yourself what you'd love to create. How would you live if you spent more time doing what you love rather than what you don't love?

CREATION AND POWER

Stressed-out is an experience of feeling powerless about some circumstance. You feel obligated to do something and feel powerless to refuse. You think that you can't say no. Or, you feel overwhelmed by obligations and responsibilities. Feeling overwhelmed is a state of helplessness. You feel that you don't have the time or ability to do what you're supposed to do. You can't get it all done on time. You feel compressed by lack of power, lack of ability, and lack of time to do something you don't want to do.

In contrast, the capacity to create empowers you. By changing your own vision of yourself from stressed-out reactor to unwanted stressors to creator of your dreams, you claim the power to replace stress with passion to create what you would love to have in your life.

Stress is reactive and creation is proactive. Stress reacts to what exists. Creation focuses your energy forward. By looking forward, you change your perspective from solving an unwanted problem into a future vision. This change of focus from the past to the future, from memories of guilt, fear, and trauma, to a vision of future possibilities empowers you. It replaces fear of the future with positive excitement about what you can create. It turns the sorrows of the past into the joys of creating what you love.

Life is the experience of beginnings and endings and constant change. This means that life is filled with opportunities for new beginnings. Whatever your circumstances, you can choose to create something because you would love to do it. By refocusing your attention, you can overcome stressful obstacles to living a happy, peaceful life:

- You can grow beyond your memories of a painful past.
- You change the present from a time of stress into a time of creation.

Making something you love is a liberating experience because it takes your mind off your problems to concentrate on what you're creating. Creating can be as complicated as building a house or as simple as arranging a bouquet of flowers. If you love what you're doing, you'll be absorbed by doing it.

FIRST-PERSON TO THIRD-PERSON

In his book, *Creating*, Robert Fritz emphasizes the distinction between first-person and third-person perspectives. He claims that a change in focus from first person to third person sets you free from the constraints of your ego so you can create what you choose:

> If you have lived your life in the first-person orientation, you can shift your point of view. It is truly to your advantage to live in the third person, because you will gain greater perception, and more of an ability to create what you want.[39]

The language of stress is typically expressed in the grammatical first person—the famed trio of *me, myself,* and *I.* "I can't do it." "I don't want to do it." "I'm overwhelmed." "It's not fair to me." The language of stress is about how some stressor is affecting you and how some person or circumstance is "making you feel" stressed-out.

If you choose to change roles from "stressed-out" to "creator," you'll gain great benefit by changing your perspective from first person to third person. When you focus on creating something that you'd love to have in your life, your attention is no longer on what a stressor is doing to you. Third-person perspective changes your focus from "me, myself, and I" to the creation itself.

Third-person language focuses on the other, whether the other is a person or a thing, rather than on your self. Love does that. It changes your focus from *me, myself,* and *I* to your creation. It's no longer all about what happens to you. Now, you focus on the object of your love.

First-time parents often change focus from first person to third person—not always—but often enough to demonstrate the kind of life change that occurs with the birth of a baby. The baby becomes the focus of attention, the wondrous little being in the center of the universe.

THINKING IN THE THIRD PERSON

Why is it valuable to change your primary focus from first person to third person when you desire to create something in your life? Creating in the third person gives you a more objective perspective than thinking of the effect on yourself. If you're focused on yourself, your emotions can interfere with your thinking about your creation. However, if you're not the center of attention, you can develop a more discerning perception of your creation than you can if it's all about you.

Creating from the perspective of the third person gives you insights and a level of objectivity that allows you to go beyond your feelings so you can think clearly about your creation. When you acknowledge that the creation isn't you, you can look at it closely, you can look at it from a distance, you can change your perspective. You're not part of the creation. If your focus is on yourself, it's impossible to get this change of perspective because you can't get outside of your self to observe your creation.

Creation isn't about the creator. It's about the creation. By seeing something as a creation, you can separate your ego from the process. You focus on what you intend to create. Creation isn't about fixing yourself. You create something because you desire it to exist. Creation also ignores any litany of faults and failures you might have experienced in the past. You're not thinking with your ego-mind that makes everything you do be about you and how you compare to others. The key component of creation is love. You create something out of love, not because you want to solve a problem.

A third-person perspective sets your energy free to create what you love rather than cope with the relentless demands of others and the constant reminders from your ego-mind of your own failures and inadequacies. A third-person perspective enables you to be passionate about the creation and dispassionate about yourself. As a creator, you don't focus on what you think is wrong with you, solving your problems, or getting approval. Rather, you focus on making something that you want to exist.

The mindset change in this transition from problem solving to creation is powerful if you can grasp it. You're creating something that is not you. You desire it to be the best you can make. You desire it to be something you love.

If your creation isn't about you, then you don't have to think about your failures. If the creation is about what you would love to have, you're not spending your time thinking about something that you don't love. When the creation is about love, it's not done with any sort of intention of getting back at someone, at redeeming yourself, or impressing others. Rather the creation is something you create because you would love to have it exist. Rather than thinking about yourself, you can focus on what you would love to create. This change of perspective is a powerful way to change your life from stressed-out to peaceful.

~

QUESTIONS TO THINK ABOUT

1. Do you speak the language of a creator or a stressed-out person?
2. Are you the doer or the direct object in your sentences?
3. Did you give up your dreams of doing great things, of going places, of making a difference in the world?
4. How would your life be different if you spent most of your time doing what you love rather than spending your time dealing with what you don't want in your life?
5. Can you imagine yourself as a creator rather than stressed-out?
6. Why is it valuable for you change your primary focus from first-person to third person when you desire to create something in your life?

Chapter 16

Thinking About Energy

Feel the power that comes from focusing on what excites you.

Oprah Winfrey

STRESS AND LIFE ENERGY

What's the role of stress in your creative process? Up to now, *stress* has been the villain, the unwanted intruder in your life, the obstacle to having and doing and being what you want. What if stress itself is essential to turn a stressed-out life into a peaceful life? To consider this question, we need to consider the connection between energy and life. What's the role of energy in your life? Do you feel energetic or do you feel depleted of energy?

Energy is power in motion. Energy is the difference between life and death. Living things move. Dead things don't. Without energy, there's no power and no motion. Without energy, there's no life.

Albert Einstein said:

Nothing happens until something moves.

Consider how often success language describes moving forward in pursuit of your goals. *Progress* means to "move forward." You're "making progress" if you keep moving forward. You're not making progress if you have "setbacks." A setback is a reversal in your process of moving forward. The language of "pursuit of your goals" conjures up the idea that you're constantly chasing after goals that are always ahead of you. This is the language of motion in a straight line. Go full speed ahead. Don't look back. Keep moving forward to succeed in life.

THE BALANCE BETWEEN OPPOSING AND COMPLEMENTARY FORCES

The wisdom of Einstein's words that nothing happens until something moves can also generate stress-producing thoughts and actions in your life. These few words omit an important truth about motion in your life. Life energy isn't motion in only one direction. The motion that makes something happen often requires motion both forwards and backwards. Life energy is a balance between opposing and complementary forces. *Opposing* means "opposite." *Complementary* means to "complete."

"Opposing" might not sound like a good idea until you stop to consider how "handy" it is for you to have opposable thumbs. Try taping your thumbs to your hands and spend a day using only your fingers. (You'll have to get help to tape each thumb to a hand.) At the end of the day—if you last that long—you can spend some time pondering the benefits of opposing and complementary forces in your life.

Let's consider another instance. We live on a huge rotating ball traveling in an elliptical orbit around and around and around the Sun. This orbit demonstrates a balance between two forces acting upon Earth. The ever-expanding energy released in the *Big Bang* pulls Earth outward. Meanwhile, the contracting force of the Sun's gravity pulls Earth toward the Sun. The result of these expanding and contracting forces on Earth keeps Earth in its elliptical orbit around the Sun. If the Sun's gravity were the only force acting on Earth, Earth would be pulled into the Sun, swallowed up, and never seen again. If the Sun's gravity were turned off, Earth would fly off in the opposite direction. In either case, life as we know it on Earth would cease. The balance between the contracting gravity of the Sun and the expanding energy from the Big Bang makes life on this Earth possible.

Still not convinced? How about your heart? Your heart is a powerful muscle. Muscles have the capacity to expand and contract. Your heart consists of two pumps with a system of valves that keeps blood flowing in one direction. Each pump has an atrium and a ventricle. An atrium receives blood from veins and a ventricle pumps blood into arteries. It's a wondrously powerful system of opposing and complementary forces that keeps blood flowing in one direction by a process of compressing and contracting. If either compression or contraction stops or is impeded in some way, your heart is in serious trouble, and your life is in jeopardy.

Eastern traditions have always recognized the necessary balance between opposing and complementary forces. *Yin and yang* describe complementary forces such as hot and cold, wet and dry, light and dark, male and female. The opposing and complementary forces are not static, unchanging states. Rather these opposing and complementary forces create a *dynamic* system. Dynamic means "power producing motion."

One more example of a complementary system of dynamic energy is the accordion. An accordion makes music as the accordionist alternately compresses and expands the bellows, which allows air to flow across the reeds. As the reeds vibrate, they produce sounds inside the body of the accordion. The player produces specific sounds by playing keys or buttons. An accordion must have this alternating compression and expansion to make music. An accordion cannot make music without dynamic movement in two directions.

THE ESSENTIAL ROLE OF STRESS

Think about the radical notion that stress is a necessary part of any creative process—with one important revision. "Stress" language is usually about what you don't want in your life. When it comes to describing the actions of your heart and your accordion, the word *stress* is often replaced by the word *compression*.

Both stress and compression squeeze. However *stress* gets the bad reputation while *compression* gets the good reputation. Hearts and accordions don't work without compression. You already know stress as the villain in your life. Do you also know that stress—under the name of compression—is essential for your life? Using the power of compression—stress—in a dynamic process is an essential part of any creative activity.

Imagine yourself as an accordion. Are you an accordion in motion or are you so compressed that you can't move? Accordions can't make music and you can't do much of anything in your life if compression becomes a static condition rather than a part of a dynamic process. Your heart continues to beat and you can play your accordion only if both opposing and complementary forces are working in harmony with each other.

FOCUS REQUIRES COMPRESSION

What's the point? Without compression—stress—you can't create what you love. Think about these words by Oprah Winfrey:

> Feel the power that comes from focusing on what excites you.

Focus requires compression. Compression focuses your energy on one objective, one goal, one activity, one process. Whatever it is, you compress your attention onto some narrowly defined object or action. If you're doing what you care about, something you want to do, something you love doing, you're not going to feel stressed by doing it, no matter how hard you work. Rather, you use the complementary forces that allow your creation to grow.

When you focus on what you're truly interested in doing, you'll be energized by it. You might feel tired, but it won't be "stressed-out tired." You'll feel the kind of tired that results when you expend yourself doing something you love doing.

The interaction of opposing and complementary forces produces dynamic power—the "power that comes from focusing on what excites you." This dynamic power is the essential difference between living a life that drains your energy and living a life that energizes you:

Consider Maya Angelou words:

> Love life, engage in it, give it all you've got. Love it with a passion, because life truly does give back, many times over, what you put into it.

The energy in your life can be measured by the amount of passion you put into it. It's not the other way around. You don't become passionate because you have energy. You have energy because you become passionate. It's difficult to tap into much energy when you're doing something you don't want to do. Passion is the fuel that turns what you do into something you care about. You gain increased power when you focus on what excites you. The more you focus on what interests you, what excites you, what you're passionate about, the more you'll become energized.

In contrast, work drains your power when you're doing something that you truly don't want to do. Life is like that. If you're just going through the motions without getting involved in what you do, it's the equivalent of draining a battery, except that it's your energy that's being drained. You'll feel stressed-out rather than energized.

Finding the balance is the challenge of any life. How do you do the essential tasks of life without exhausting your life energy? How do you energize yourself as you do necessary work to take care of yourself and those who depend on you without draining your passion for life?

COMPLAINING

What can you do to stop draining your energy? One powerful choice concerns complaining. You surely know people who are chronic complainers. You see a chronic complainer coming and you know that you're in for the latest grievance. Have you ever met a happy complainer? Of course not. A chronic complainer is perpetually unhappy about something or other.

No matter what the situation, they'll find something to complain about. Chronic complainers become toxic in any environment. They can sour the mood faster than anything you know. These are the people you don't want to see, because you know you're about to hear another set of complaints about what "they" did or didn't do.

Chronic complaining extracts a toll from the complainer. They don't feel well—and will complain about how bad they feel. Chronic complainers also drain your energy. If you have chronic complainers in your life, it's worth asking what kind of energy toll they are exacting from you.

What if you realize that you're the one doing the constant complaining? If so, it's time to acknowledge how much constant complaining depletes your energy. Complaining about your situation without doing something to change it is almost always a waste of time and more significantly, a waste of your energy. Energy is a precious resource. Complaining can become a self-destructive habit that does you no good.

Complaining effectively turns attention from what you're doing to the actions of some external force. Whether it's someone else, the weather, or unwanted circumstances, if you're complaining about something, you're expressing your own unwillingness or ability to deal with it. Dealing with it might mean accepting the reality that no one is responsible for the snow storm that kept you stuck in traffic and late getting to work.

The more you find the reasons for your discontent outside of yourself, the less you will look at yourself to discover how you can be productive and happy in almost any situation. Complaining is wasted energy unless your complaints are addressed to the one who can do something about it. Otherwise, you're venting emotions that express your own belief that you are powerless, or that someone else is responsible for how happy or unhappy you feel at any given moment.

When you spend your energy on some action that doesn't replenish your own energy supply, you're draining your own life battery. It's expenditure of energy in one direction, with nothing to replenish it.

Constant complaining over a circumstance in life can't energize you. In contrast, when you spend your energy in some sort of creative, productive, enjoyable action, you replenish your energy. You're plugged into the source of your energy, which is your passion for what you're doing.

BEING BUSY

We live in a world of busy people. People are too busy to cook. Too busy to read. Too busy to play. Too busy to enjoy themselves. Most people are busy, but the real question is, busy doing what? And more significantly, being busy to what purpose?

How much of your life energy do you expend by being busy? What's the purpose of your busyness? Are you being creative and productive? Are you busy working on a specific goal that's important to you? Or are you busy being busy? Being busy is a frequent way to get derailed from what's important to you. Analyze how you spend your time. You can make an inventory of the activities that keep you so busy. How many do you think you *have to* do? How many do you *love* to do?

Some activities deplete your energy. What activities leave you feeling depressed, discouraged, and drained? Are they things you do because you're required to do them by your job? Are they housework tasks that you do because they're necessary? Paying bills? Shopping? Cleaning? Commuting to work? Are they social clubs that no longer interest you, but you attend because you joined a long time ago?

You have only so much time and life energy to spend. Are you spending your time and energy on what refreshes you, inspires you, energizes you, or something that leaves you numb and drained?

WHAT ACTIVITIES ENERGIZE YOU?

What activities energize you? What do you do that leaves you feeling refreshed, satisfied, and in a good mood? What about it produces the good feelings? Is it the activity itself? Is it the people you do the activity with? Is it physical activity outside? Hiking in a beautiful place? Shopping? Going out for lunch with a friend? Working on a hobby? Some part of your work? When do you feel better after doing something than you felt before you started?

You can use these questions to monitor how your energy fluctuates between activities. If you feel energized by some activity, how can you arrange your life to do it more often? If your job is draining your energy, what can you change to energize yourself?

RELATIONSHIPS AND ENERGY

Consider the people in your life. What people energize you? What people drain your energy? Which are the ones you're glad to see and which ones are those you want to avoid if possible? If this is your reaction, it's a good possibility that you already know the difference between energy-boosting people and those who have the opposite effect. The next step is to be resolute and determine what to do about the energy drainers. Are they people you can't avoid in your life? Or are they people you would rather not include in your circle of friends, family, and acquaintances?

You can also consider exactly how the energizers are different from the de-energizers. What do they do or not do? What do the de-energizers do that drain your energy? Honesty with yourself is important here. Someone might be a longtime friend, but it might be time to let that friend go. What's the cost to you in keeping a negative person in your life? On the other hand, how can you spend more time with the people who lift you up and energize you? Old habits can be hard to break and relationships can be even harder to change.

INTENTION AND ENERGY

What kind of energy do you put into the world? Are you someone who raises the energy level of a room when you enter it or are you someone who drains energy?

An effective way to raise your own energy level is to offer a silent blessing every time you go into a space. For example, every time you go through a doorway, you make a silent declaration of peace to be present in the place.

A blessing intends the best for someone. Blessing doesn't have to be tied to any sort of religious belief or ceremony. Rather, intending blessing for others is an act of consciousness on your part. If you enter a space, you offer a blessing. You can do it when you enter rooms, buses, stores, houses, or any other place that involves passing through a doorway. You don't do anything obvious. No signs, rituals, or incantations. You simply declare a silent blessing for the wellbeing of all who are in that space.

Does it make a difference? It might not make a difference for anyone else, but it will make a difference for you. This simple intention will energize you. If you offer a silent blessing for the wellbeing of everyone who's in a space you enter, you'll feel better. It's a simple thought-action that can also work wonders to relieve you of your stressed-out feelings. Try it and find out for yourself. What have you got to lose except feeling stressed-out?

How do you turn stressed-out frustration into positive, effective, unstoppable determination? You do it by focusing on your vision of what you desire to create. Positive determination to make some thing happen is more powerful than complaining about what you don't want in your life. Positive determination changes you from helpless recipient of injustice from others to active doer in the service your dreams. You can't generate energy by feeling powerless. You create energy by your determination to create what you love.

~

QUESTIONS TO THINK ABOUT

1. How is stress itself essential to turn a stressed-out life into a peaceful life?

2. What's the role of energy in your life? Do you feel energetic or do you feel depleted of energy?

3. What's the benefit of focusing your energy on one objective, one goal, one activity, one process?

4. How much passion do you put into your life?

5. What can you do to stop draining your life energy?

6. What's the impact of complaining on your life energy?

7. What's the purpose of your busyness? Are you being creative and productive? Are you busy being busy?

8. Are you spending your time and energy on what refreshes you, inspires you, energizes you, or something that leaves you numb and drained?

9. What activities energize you?

10. What people energize you? What people drain your energy?

11. What kind of energy do you put into the world?

PART VI

THINKING ABOUT
YOUR PEACEFUL LIFE

Chapter 17

Thinking About Serenity

God, give us grace to accept with serenity the things that cannot be changed, courage to change the things that should be changed, and the wisdom to distinguish the one from the other.

Original wording of the Serenity Prayer by
Reinhold Niebuhr

STRESS AND SERENITY

Reinhold Niebuhr's Serenity Prayer was adopted as the official prayer of Alcoholics Anonymous. The best known form of the prayer is:

God, grant me the serenity to accept the things I cannot change,

The courage to change the things I can,

And the wisdom to know the difference.[40]

Whether you use them as a prayer or as a wise adage, these words offer profound wisdom about dealing with stressors in your life. Once again, it's important to differentiate between powerful external stressors and stressors created by your own thoughts, feelings, and reactions to ordinary life circumstances. Whether or not you succumb to a particular stressor comes down to knowing the difference between what you can change and what you can't change.

For example, you can't change the torrential rainstorm that is washing out the road. You can change the way you think about the torrential rainstorm that is washing out the road. You can accept with serenity that you can't change it and you don't take it personally.

Remember the unhappy young man at the San Francisco fireworks. He made himself miserable by complaining that no one was doing anything about the fog. The fog was something that no one could change at that time and in that place. The path of serenity was to accept that as fact. The path to stressed-out was to expect someone to change what no one could change. He chose the path to stressed-out rather than the path of serenity by wanting someone to change what could not be changed.

WHAT IS SERENITY?

What is serenity? The English word *serene* is derived from the Latin *serenus,* meaning "peaceful, calm, clear." Serenity is state of calmness and acceptance of current circumstances.

Serenity is the equivalent to floating peacefully in the ocean. As a young child growing up on Cape Cod, I learned to float before I learned to swim. The secret of floating is to lie on your back with your arms outstretched and allow yourself to be carried by the waves. If you allow the ocean to carry you, the waves won't wash over your face and you won't be pulled under.

As a five or six-year old, I used to watch as one of "the summer people"—the Cape Cod designation for tourists in those days—tried to teach a child how to float. As soon as the child felt a wave touch her face, she would resist it, and end up with a faceful of water. I felt so superior because I knew the secret. I wouldn't be swamped if I let the waves carry me. That's still the best lesson I have ever learned about serenity. Don't resist the force that's supporting you. Simply lie back and trust the waves to carry you.

THE SECRET OF SERENITY

The secret of serenity is to know when to float and when to swim. This wisdom to know the difference between the things you can change and the things you can't relates directly to how much stress you experience in your life. All kinds of events happen in this world that have nothing to do with you personally but they affect you in some way.

Stressed-out doesn't just happen to you. Stressed-out is self-created when people get upset over circumstances that are beyond anyone's control. You see it in traffic jams. An accident ahead has blocked the road. No one can move. Then someone starts blowing the horn in anger and frustration. No amount of blowing the horn is going to clear the wrecked vehicles any faster. All it does is create more stress in the horn blower and annoy everyone else.

The futility of getting angry in such a situation is obvious. Other situations might not be quite as obvious, but you can always check yourself. Are you stressing yourself because you're frustrated about a situation that no one can change at that moment? Such frustration serves no purpose. If you realize that you're doing the equivalent of blowing your horn when the traffic can't go anywhere, you can choose serenity over stress by waiting calmly until the problem is resolved.

How do you develop serenity in potentially stressful situations? Simone Weil made an important distinction in her words:

> In struggling against anguish one never produces serenity;
> the struggle against anguish only produces a new form of
> anguish.

If you can't change something—really can't—then struggling against it is worse than useless.

Struggling is resistance to what is. *Anguish* is extreme "suffering, grief, or pain." It's directly related to the word *anger* from the Greek *ankhein*. Anger means to "irritate, annoy, or provoke." The root meaning of anger is "tight, painfully constricted, and painful." These definitions share the sense of constriction that defines the experience of stress.

What's the relationship between serenity and your desire to change your life? Serenity begins by accepting current reality as it is, but serenity is not the same as resignation. Resignation accepts current reality without any hope of being able to change anything. The mindset of resignation is: "This is the way things are and I can't do anything about it." Ending the struggle in situations you can't change isn't the same as feeling resigned to your fate. Serenity isn't helpless surrender but willing acceptance of current reality. From this calm, empowering perspective, you can consider the difference between what you can change and what you can't change.

SERENITY AND PEACE

What are the differences between *serenity* and *peacefulness,* between *serenity* and *peace?* Each word has a slew of synonyms and antonyms. Although common speech often uses them interchangeably, you can gain great insight when you think about the basic difference between them:

- Peace is absence of conflict in a relationship.
- Serenity is personal calmness in a situation.

Peace concerns relationships with others. Peace is the antonym of *war*. War is about conflict. Conflict means "to strike together." Conflicts can range from simple disagreements to outright violence. The conflict can be a real war—a military conflict. It can also be conflict with others—whether as individuals, families, tribes, businesses, or anything else that pits people against each other. The language of war is sometimes used to describe inner conflict within yourself. Peace is the absence of war, the absence of conflict. Peace defines a condition of harmony in relationships with others.

In contrast to the word peace, *serenity* describes what is happening within you, not what is happening in an external relationship. Serenity is *composure, patience, stillness, calmness, tranquility, peace of mind.* It's the opposite of *agitation, anxiety, apprehension.* All of these words describe how you feel about yourself, not your relationship with anyone else.

SERENITY AND STRESS

Serenity is your most effective antidote against stressors in your life. The difference between feeling stressed-out and serene is calmness. Stress describes mental activity that is too much, too fast. Feeling stressed-out is fundamentally a lack of focus on doing one thing calmly. Stress-creating thoughts tell you: "I have more than I can handle. I have too much to do. I don't know what to do about it."

The difference between stressed-out and calmness is the difference between water boiling in kettle and water in a gently flowing river. In the kettle, bubbles begin to form as the heat rises. The hotter the water, the more bubbles rise to the surface and become more agitated over time. More and more bubbles form until the kettle is filled with roiling water. Stress increases with rapid movement. In contrast, calmness describes the river water flowing placidly in one direction without the convection currents of boiling water. The water is moving but it's not frantic. The water flows at its gentle pace to get where it's going.

Serenity takes much of the melodrama out of your life. If you're serene, you can make decisions without obsessing over what to do. You can what you do calmly rather than with panic.

Viggo Mortensen offers these words of wisdom about calmness:

> One of the best pieces of advice I ever got was from a horse master. He told me to go slow to go fast. I think that applies to everything in life. We live as though there aren't enough hours in the day but if we do each thing calmly and carefully we will get it done quicker and with much less stress.

Serenity is the result of doing what you do calmly rather than in a rushed and anxious state of mind. Serenity counteracts the self-induced stress that reacts to every circumstance as a catastrophe in the making. Agitated people treat everything as a big deal. Anything that happens is an occasion to go crazy with worry, and in the process, to disturb everyone else.

Even in the presence of stressors, serene people don't succumb to the tendency to make mountains out of molehills and to turn decisions about minor things into big deals. Serenity means fewer snap judgments and rash decisions. Serenity leads to decisions made with wisdom, care, and the intention of the best possible outcome.

PEACE OF MIND COMES FROM YOU

Serenity. Calmness. Peace of mind. They all describe the same condition. Contrary to claims of advertisers that some product will give you peace of mind, peace of mind isn't a condition that anyone can give you. You give yourself peace of mind by how you react to circumstances in your life. You create peace of mind when you're willing to trust in yourself, trust in your circumstances, and trust that all will be well.

Trust doesn't mean that you stop doing due diligence when you buy something or entrust another person to do something for you. You expect the best even as you plan for the worst. Peace of mind is when you decide that it's not worth getting yourself upset in advance, based on your fears about what might happen. Peace of mind is when you don't let potential problems ruin your present.

WHAT YOU CAN CONTROL

Why do bad things happen to you? If you believe that all that happens in the world is the result of God's will for your life—no matter how heinous or terrible—then it's your responsibility to accept what happens. If you believe some New Age claims that you cause everything that happens to you—no matter how heinous or terrible—then it's your responsibility to learn some lesson about your cosmic self. In both cases, you believe that whatever happens is personal and designed to teach you some lesson.

By definition, a belief is:

> Confidence in the truth or existence of something not immediately susceptible to rigorous proof.

You can't prove a belief. You can only believe it. Wherever you stand on any belief/non-belief continuum, you can evaluate how your beliefs affect your peace of mind. Whatever the theological, spiritual, or metaphysical implications of all of this, you can control your conduct. You can choose what you say and what you do.

Benjamin Disraeli said:

> Circumstances are beyond human control, but your conduct is in your own power.

This difference between circumstances and your conduct can determine how you react to stressors in your life. How do you react to circumstances? Are you a raving manic, are you sulking because you can't get your way, or are you able to act with dignity, compassion, courage, and honor in any situation.

In his book, *Flow*, Mihaly Csikszentmihalyi offers particular words of wisdom about why people are so chronically unhappy:

> The foremost reason that happiness is so hard to achieve is that the universe was not designed with the comfort of human beings in mind.[41]

Or to express this reality in different terms, everything that happens to you is not about you. Whatever truth exists in claims that God did it to teach you a lesson or that your higher self did it to teach you a lesson, it's worth pondering how much it costs you in stress and worry to take personally everything that happens in your life. Maybe things just happen.

A LIFE OF PEACE

You can replace much of the stress in your life with calmness by how you think about what happens in your life. Whether you call it *peace, peace of mind, inner peace, peacefulness, calmness,* or *serenity,* the result is the same. You replace constant worry with a belief that all is well. With this attitude, you can experience *shalom.*

Shalom is the Hebrew word translated as *peace.* However, *shalom* is a rich word with a depth of meaning beyond the idea of peace. Shalom is a relationship word. Shalom is more than the absence of war; shalom is the experience of wholeness in relationship to others and your world. Above all, shalom is the intention of wellbeing. Wellbeing is not just the absence of conflict; it refers to the fullness of life. It's not just about how you feel. Shalom is the intention of wellbeing for others. Shalom envisions a time when all is well, when neither pain nor struggle exists.

Feeling stressed-out is the opposite of shalom, of peace, of serenity. A stressed-out mind cannot see beyond the present to imagine a different future. The essential insight that makes the difference between stressed-out and serene is to know that this moment is not the end. No matter how bad it is right now, this too shall pass.

~

QUESTIONS TO THINK ABOUT

1. Do you accept with serenity the difference between what you can change and what you can't change?
2. How can you develop serenity in potentially stressful situations?
3. What's the relationship between serenity and your desire to change your life?
4. How do you react to circumstances?
5. Do you take personally everything that happens in your life?
6. How can you replace much of the stress in your life with calmness?

Chapter 18

Thinking About Grace

Grace is the absence of everything that indicates pain or difficulty, hesitation or incongruity.

William Hazlitt

STRESS AND GRACE

Although William Hazlitt's definition of grace doesn't use the word *stress*, he is describing grace as the opposite of stress. Instead of writing that "grace is the absence of everything that indicates pain or difficulty, hesitation or incongruity," he could have written "grace is the absence of stress."

The word *grace* has a range of meanings in English, originating in its ancestors, the Latin *gratia* and the Old French *grace*. The Latin connotations included "favor, esteem, regard, pleasing quality, good will, gratitude." Old French meanings included "pardon, divine grace, mercy; favor, thanks, elegance, virtue." The English word *grace* inherited all of these wide-ranging definitions from its Latin and Old French ancestors. What meaning of grace can best enable you to turn stressed-out into peaceful?

The connotation of *grace as favor* is the meaning used by Christian theologians to develop a theology of grace. In Christian theology, grace refers to God's forgiveness and acceptance of you despite your sins. This is the connotation behind such statements such as: "There but for the grace of God go I." This definition makes grace an undeserved gift you receive rather than a quality you possess. This is not the perspective of grace that I intend here.

Rather, let's focus on the particular connotation of grace as *a pleasing quality*. This meaning of grace refers to gracefulness, elegance, ease, and fluidity of motion. This is the grace of the elegant figure skaters who dazzle you with what looks like effortless flow as they glide across the ice.

This is also the meaning of grace in Hans Christian Andersen's well-known story, "The Ugly Duckling." Of all of the birds, the white swan is the one most known for its gracefulness as it glides through the water, with its long neck arched ever so elegantly.[42]

EASE

One of the primary qualities of grace is *ease*. Ease is not just about moving gracefully, ease is also about living gracefully. Does this mean that living with *ease* is *easy?* In contemporary English usage—as frequently happens—the original distinctions between words got lost in ordinary usage. *Ease* and *easy* both derived from Old French with different connotations. *Ease* meant "mitigate, alleviate, relieve from pain or care." *Easy* meant "without difficulty." Ease describes a state of mind—living life without pain or worry. Easy describes activity—living life with minimal effort.

This distinction demonstrates why you can live a life of ease that is not easy. Although most of us want life to be easy, most accomplishments worth doing are far from easy. Ease is often the result of hard work. In the case of ice skaters, the fluidity of motion and gracefulness that look so effortless result from years of dedicated practice. Ease on the ice means getting up early, day after day, to practice in cold rinks before going off to school. It means working on the same moves again and again to reach mastery. None of it is inherently easy.

This fluidity of motion and gracefulness produces what Mihaly Csikszentmihalyi named *flow* in his extraordinary book, *Flow: The Psychology of Optimal Experience*. He defines flow as:

> The state in which people are so involved in an activity that nothing else seems to matter; the experience itself is so enjoyable that people will do it even at great cost, for the sheer sake of doing it.[43]

A Broader Definition of Grace

Gracefulness is obvious when it refers to movement of your body. All of your body parts work together flawlessly and seamlessly. In contrast, stress demonstrates lack of grace in motion. Clumsiness, awkwardness, and stiffness are signs of a body under stress. A stressed-out person often stumbles, trips, falls, and drops things. Stress can turn you into the bull in the china shop, the dancer with two left feet who manages to step on your partner's foot, or the clumsy person who spills hot coffee on your guest's lap. Whatever the inner cause of your stress, your body will give you away as it bumbles and stumbles its way through life. Such lack of gracefulness is a clear sign that you're not at home in yourself.

The definition of grace goes beyond the movement of your body. Grace also applies to your sense of identity. Are you free to move?

"Free to move" goes beyond the literal sense of moving your body to describe your freedom to move in a metaphorical sense. If you feel stressed-out by your life circumstances, you're compressed in a life that's too small for you. Rather than dancing gracefully on a dance floor, or skating elegantly on a rink, you're trying to dance in a closet or skate on the ice of a child's wading pool. Your stressed-out feelings reveal that you don't have enough room to glide freely through your life because you're stuck in a space that's too small for you. Lack of ease demonstrates your belief that life is inherently hard and full of struggle, the belief that you're confined in a life filled with one crisis after another, one catastrophe after another, and you don't have enough room to move.

STRESS AND IDENTITY

The story of the *ugly duckling* offers profound insight into the difference between external body changes and internal mindset changes. Although the body of the ugly duckling changes over the course of the story, the ugly duckling's life-changing insight is not about the transformation of his body. Rather, it's a story about discovery of his true identity. The ugly ducking was always a swan. However, he didn't know he was a swan. He was hatched by a duck, called a duck by those around him, and treated cruelly because he didn't look like a duck.

The cause of stress in the story is he didn't know his true identity. Apparently those around him didn't know either. They treated him cruelly because he was different from the other ducklings. Since he had no way of knowing that they were wrong about him, he believed what they said about him.

No one in the story told him that he was a swan. It's true that the young swan didn't look the baby ducks in the nest and he didn't look like the beautiful swans flying overhead. Why would a baby swan look like a baby duck? Why would a young swan look like an adult swan? Babies and children are not adults. None of us start out looking like the adults we become.

When the ugly duckling finally saw his reflection in clear water after a harsh winter, he discovered his true identity. He knew who he was for the first time in his life. He wasn't a duck. He was a swan. He had lived a miserable, stressed-out life because he wasn't aware that he was a swan. The reflection of himself as a swan turned stressed-out into peaceful.

This little story is so well-loved because it's rich with meaning about self-awareness, about being tormented by the cruel and flat-out wrong comments by other people, and about the life-changing impact of a vision of yourself as you truly are.

PERCEPTION OF YOUR IDENTITY

How do the differences between graceful and stressed-out affect your perception of your identity? Stressed-out reveals a state of mind built on a sense of being fragmented. The busyness of your life can lead to fragmenting yourself. You don't have time to glide through your life because you're always sprinting from one place to another, often arriving late. Life becomes a long to-do list that you can never manage to finish. No matter what you do, the list grows longer day-by-day. You can never catch up.

Much self-help work reinforces the perception that life is one long to-do list. You have to work on yourself, make lists of what you did wrong, what you have to do, what you didn't get done. It's a nitpicker's guide to "fixing what's wrong with you." Such a perspective breeds insecurity, unhappiness, and anxiety. Living your life as an endless series of stressed-out sprints to do all of the things you "have to do" blocks a vision of other possibilities for your life.

ACCEPTANCE OF YOUR WHOLENESS

Grace is a state of mind. A graceful life begins with a change in perspective about your identity. The unhappy, tormented young swan who thought he was an ugly duckling finally saw his true self. The swan experienced a state of grace only when he came home to himself. This is the potential for all of us. The stress-filled journey can turn into a graceful life of ease when you finally see yourself as yourself.

Grace is a state of mind built on a deep sense of being whole. Wholeness is a sense of being undivided within yourself. When you feel whole, you're at home in your life, at home in your body, at home in your sense of who you are. You experience wholeness when you truly accept yourself as you are.

Does this mean that you're flawless? That you never make a mistake? That you can do no wrong? This is not what wholeness means. It's not a moral inventory or a personality test. To be whole means that you do not hold any part of yourself in contempt. You're not at war with parts of your self. You're a whole person and you don't attempt to get rid of any part of yourself.

Wholeness also means that you already have what you need within you. Wholeness produces graceful motion, graceful ease, and graceful thoughts. Such a sense of wholeness can come only from seeing that you're not a flawed being who needs to be transformed into something else. In your liberating vision of yourself, you're not a problem to be solved. Problem solving makes something unwanted go away. You don't get rid of parts of yourself. You don't attempt to amputate parts of yourself to accord with some notion of being flawless. Rather you own all that you are. Grace comes from ending the long struggle to suppress parts of you to fit someone else's definition of who you are, or who you are supposed to be.

A sense of wholeness begins when you have a grace-filled vision of your identity. When you can see yourself as a whole being, you'll see a swan gliding gracefully through the water, not a tormented and awkward ugly duckling. Grace is a state of being at home as a complete being.

GRACE AND YOUR IDENTITY CREATED BY TRAUMA

William Hazlitt's definition of grace is particularly insightful because he includes the word pain as a symptom of lack of grace.

> Grace is the absence of everything that indicates pain or difficulty, hesitation or incongruity.

In addition to any kind of physical healing that must occur to heal trauma, a perspective of grace is an essential aspect of healing trauma because it allows you to see yourself as a whole being. This is not the grace of Christian theology that refers to God's forgiveness and acceptance of you *despite* your sins. Christian theology can be surprisingly short on solutions to trauma as a result of injury from accidents or harm inflicted upon you by others.

The kind of grace that heals you gives you a vision of yourself as a whole being. It's the experience of the swan who thought he was a duck. The vision of himself as whole and beautiful was enough to heal his fractured identity. The ugly duckling comes to a point in the story when he actually expresses such joy in his experience of seeing himself as he is that he doesn't regret any of his sufferings.

RESTORING WHOLENESS

Life is about motion, the constant flow of energy. When you feel whole, you're able to flow through your life with ease. Instead of attempting to let go of the part of you that's stuck in the trauma of the past, you focus on putting yourself back together again. You see yourself as whole, rather than fragmented. You see your life as a movie rather than a snapshot frozen in time at the moment of greatest hurt. Instead of separating yourself from the wounded part, you welcome it as part of your whole life, but you don't let it define your life.

Grace is about putting it all together. To own the part of you that endured, not to abandon it. This is the power of grace, the capacity to make yourself whole by reclaiming the power of flow in your life. How do you do this? You do it by seeing yourself as whole in a process of letting go and holding on.

ENDING THE STRUGGLE

The experience of grace involves both letting go and holding on. Remember Havelock Ellis's claim:

All the art of living lies in a fine mingling of letting go and holding on.

The experience of grace involves both letting go and holding on.

- You let go of your belief that you are unworthy.
- You let go of the belief that you have to seek outside of yourself to fill the gaps, mend the wounds, or approve your right to live, to be happy, to enjoy your life.
- You let go of the endless struggle to remake yourself so that others will approve of you.
- You let go of the belief that you have to fix your supposed flaws.
- You let go of your identity shaped by the belief that you were damaged beyond repair.

What do you hold on to? You hold on to the part that was traumatized. Why? Because it's part of you. You make yourself whole by welcoming the part of you that was hurt and yet continued to persevere. You become fully present in your life as you are.

Ponder deeply the words of Jon Kabat-Zinn:

All of the suffering, stress, and addiction comes from not realizing you already are what you are looking for.

It's a particularly human pathology that we are forever trying to change ourselves to be acceptable to others. The key to wholeness is to come to the point of being acceptable to yourself. You're already whole. You aren't on a quest to find some hidden part of yourself. You don't need approval to live your life. You don't have to earn it. You don't have to metamorphose into something or someone else.

Rather, you reach a point where you see that you're already complete in yourself. Wholeness is not about being flawless. It's about liberation from your belief that you're a defective being. Wholeness results from reaching a state of acceptance and love for yourself as yourself. This is a state of grace.

A NEW VISION OF YOUR FUTURE

Liberating change in your life requires a new vision. The future looks bleak if all you can imagine is a future that is nothing more than the same struggle to survive in a hostile world. You can't be any happier than you are now until you see yourself from a perspective of grace rather than stress.

Only the perspective of grace enables you to see your whole self. The young swan believed he was a duck until he could see for himself that he was actually a swan. You can't trust your vision of yourself to what other people say about you. It's up to you to see yourself as whole.

A new vision of the future from the perspective of grace turns fear into trust. Fear is a constant feeling when you feel vulnerable, unwanted, unsafe, and flawed. Grace changes that. When you truly see that you're already whole, you can trust that you already have all you need to live a whole and complete life. You don't need to seek outside of yourself for something that's missing. You don't have to seek approval from people who are incapable of seeing you as you are. You have all you need within you. Most of all, to see yourself as whole means that you can be truly happy as yourself as you turn a stressed-out life into a grace-filled peaceful life.

~

QUESTIONS TO THINK ABOUT

1. Do you experience ease in your life?

2. How do the differences between graceful and stressed-out affect your perception of your identity?

3. Do you feel fragmented?

4. Do you feel undivided within yourself?

5. Can you let go of your belief that you are unworthy?.

6. Can you let go of the belief that you have to seek outside of yourself to become whole?

7. Can you let go of the endless struggle to remake yourself so that others will approve of you?

8. Can you let go of the belief that you have to fix your supposed flaws?.

9. Can you let go of your identity shaped by the belief that you were damaged beyond repair?

Chapter 19

Thinking About
Your Life Journey

It is good to have an end to journey toward, but it is
the journey that matters in the end.

Ursula K. Le Guin

YOUR LIFE JOURNEY

Life is a journey. Life is the moving walkway in the airport. Whether
you move or not, the walkway will move you forward and dump you
off at the end. You can't stay where you are. Just as the walkway
comes to an end, whatever your phase of life right now will also come
to an end. Walking backwards on the walkway to hold you in place is
possible in the airport. It's not possible in real life. In life, there's only
one direction. Ahead.

Your journey will take you through all kinds of experiences.
Some will be wonderful. Some will be painful. Some will excite you.
Some will bore you. Some will be easy. Some will challenge you.
What's required of you is to keep moving forward.

INERTIA

Although life isn't static, a primary characteristic of a stressed-out life
is inertia. Merriam-Webster defines inertia as:

Lack of movement or activity especially when movement or
activity is wanted or needed.

Even if you know it's time to move on, time to change, time to do
something different, inertia can be a powerful force to overcome.

Remember that Albert Einstein said "nothing happens until
something moves." Inertia robs you of the essential characteristic of
all living creatures. Living creatures move. The world keeps moving,
whether you do or not. Doing something requires action. If you're
feeling too stressed-out to do anything, ask yourself what you can do
to overcome your inertia.

Isaac Newton's "Three Laws of Motion" describe the
interrelationship between an object, forces acting on the object, and
the motion of the object. The First Law is particularly relevant here.
Since Newton published the laws in Latin, the specific English words
used to describe these three laws vary depending on the reference.
Here are two contemporary statements of the First Law of Motion.
The first is more typical of physics textbooks. The second is simpler:

- When viewed in an inertial reference frame, an object
  either remains at rest or continues to move at a constant
  velocity, unless acted upon by an external force.[44]
- An object at rest will remain at rest unless acted on by an
  unbalanced force. An object in motion continues in
  motion with the same speed and in the same direction
  unless acted upon by an unbalanced force.[46]

The second source also describes the First Law of Motion as the
"Law of Inertia." Stress seems to operate according to its own Law of
Inertia. Sometimes your stress keeps you stuck in inertia. Feeling

stressed-out can define your life as "lack of movement or activity especially when movement or activity is wanted or needed."[47]

But even in a state of inertia, change is inexorable. Whether or not you stop moving, the moving walkway called life won't stop. Your life will change somehow. The question is whether you're going to succumb to the powerful force of inertia or whether you're going to be the force that gets you moving again.

Surely you have heard the adage, "Move it or lose it." Moving on means packing up and leaving the familiar behind when you're no longer growing, no longer changing, no longer interested in what you're doing. Boredom is a powerful clue that it's time to get moving.

Inertia is your greatest enemy to living a full and vibrant life. Overcoming inertia often means you set out on a new journey. We're a species with legs. We're meant to move. Whether you set out on a real journey to a different place or a journey to a different mindset, your journey will take you to a different life.

LIFE ON EARTH

Life on Earth is about constant change. Nothing is static in a living, moving, ever-changing planet. Many of the changes on Earth are measured in years, epochs, eons. Other changes are more frequent. We see changes in the winds and tides, we see the seasons change, we see the Sun rising and setting in different areas of the sky through the year. We also experience personal changes throughout our lives, as we change over time. The inevitability of constant change provides hope for anyone who feels stuck. Whatever your current situation, it won't always be this way. Something will change.

Inevitable, constant change is both good news and potentially distressing news. Wherever you are right now, whatever you have, whoever you are, you'll change. A dominant characteristic of feeling stressed-out is the belief that the current situation is hopeless. The good news is that stressors also change. Change is inevitable.

Your life has distinguishable phases. Infancy. Childhood. Adulthood. You experience stages of education. Kindergarten. Elementary school. Junior high. High school. College. You experience stages of work. Part time. Full time. Retired. You experience stages of relationships to other people. Being a child. Being a parent. Being a grandparent. Being a student. Being a teacher. Being unemployed. Being employed. Taking care of yourself. Taking care of others. Being dependent on the care of others. This is life. Birth and death. Beginnings and endings. Life is an endless series of phases, seasons, stages, and changes.

TIME FOR A JOURNEY

Are you willing to let your life unfold as a journey? A journey is about discovery. Going on a journey is not the same as being a tourist with a defined itinerary. Journeys are often quests with no clear pathway and no clear destination point. The fearful will stay at home. The adventurous will eagerly go on journeys.

What's *your* journey? That's the question, isn't it? If you knew ahead of time, it wouldn't be a journey. Journeys aren't laid out ahead of time. Journeys are full of surprises. Unexpected events. Turns in the road. Roadblocks. Detours. If you knew the route ahead of time, your life would be a tourist trip, where someone laid out an itinerary and you go from place to place according to a schedule. Tourist trips are not likely to change you much. Journeys will always change you.

It's time to move on when you begin to feel stagnant. Stagnation is another characteristic of inertia. Stagnation produces the swamp that becomes more and more stagnant over time because the fresh water no longer flows. People also become stagnant in their jobs as they go through the motions of the same old routine with no flow of fresh ideas, fresh insights, fresh passions, fresh interests. Especially for older people, it's easy to become stagnant. To settle in. To wait for the end.

How will you know if it's time to move on? You'll know if you feel stuck, stagnant, stultified. You'll know if you have a nagging discontent that you need to be doing something else. Not that you *want* to do it, but that you *need* to do it. You have an urgency. A sense that you are being *called* to something. The idea of calling can be fraught with religious and spiritual ideas. It doesn't have to be so fraught. You know that you can do something more meaningful than what you are doing. Sometimes, people confuse being busy with doing something meaningful. What can you do that matters to you?

Whatever your beliefs, consider that some part of you—whether you call it your inner self, your sensitive self, your higher self, your authentic self—some part of you believes you're *meant* to do something. "Meant to do" doesn't have to be any more complicated than the sense that you're not doing anything that engages your spirit. What have you dreamed of doing? What do you have an urgent desire to do? What can you do that allows you to use your creativity? If you're feeling such urgency, ask yourself how much of your stressed-out state of mind results from spending the time of your life doing unimportant things that don't matter to you.

What about planning? Planning is useful because it requires you to think about what matters to you. However, you can't control everything that might happen. You can intend to go somewhere but outer circumstances change everything. Unexpected events happen. Storms and catastrophes. Wars and terrorist attacks. Fires and floods. Illnesses and accidents. Deaths of people you love.

In 1957, Allen Saunders wrote: "Life is what happens to us while we are making other plans." John Lennon made the phrase famous in his song "Beautiful Boy" as "life is what happens while you're making other plans." [47]

INTUITION

Once again, we come back to self-trust and intuition. Intuition can be a reliable source of information about knowing what your next steps are. Perhaps you're aware of your intuitive insights, and willing to take them seriously. Perhaps you've never paid much attention to the flashes of insights, of hunches, of tiny thoughts that come to your mind that somehow feel different from your other thoughts. In either case, you can trust that you already know more than you realize by paying attention to your intuition. This is especially true if you have been called "too sensitive" throughout your life. Pay particular attention to your intuition if you're feeling stressed-out and want your life to be different.

Many people are far more sensitive than they realize although most of us learn to ignore those flashes of insight. Insights can be disparaged as "women's intuition" or ridiculed as figments of your imagination. If you're willing to trust that you're aware of much more than your conscious mind knows, your intuitions can speak to you clearly.

THE PATH MADE BY WALKING

In his poem, "The Road Not Taken," Robert Frost wrote about making a life journey on the "less traveled by" road:

> Two roads diverged in a wood, and I —
>
> I took the one less traveled by,
>
> And that has made all the difference.[48]

Robert Frost's poem refers to the road "less traveled by." The Spanish poet, Antonio Machado, goes beyond the idea of following any existing path. Rather, you create your path as you walk it:

> Traveler, your footprints
>
> Are the path and nothing more;
>
> Traveler, there is no path,
>
> The path is made by walking.
>
> By walking the path is made
>
> And when you look back
>
> You'll see a road
>
> Never to be trodden again.
>
> Traveler, there is no path,
>
> Only trails across the sea...[49]

Your life is your own unique journey. No one can make it for you and no will ever travel the same path again. It's up to you to find your way, whatever that way may be, to trust that you are being led by something—God, spirit, your intuition, your higher knowing, your authentic self, your dream—whatever you call it, your journey is yours to create.

Persistence is essential for your life journey. The often cited quotation by Calvin Coolidge identifies the need for persistence:

> Nothing in this world can take the place of persistence. Talent will not; nothing is more common than unsuccessful people with talent. Genius will not. Unrewarded genius is almost a proverb. Education will not. The world is full of educated derelicts. Persistence and determination alone are omnipotent. The slogan press on has solved and always will solve the problems of the human race.

Despite the temptations to quit, persistence urges you to press on rather than to give up, to keep moving especially when you feel stressed-out. If you feel stressed-out, you're squeezed into a space that's too small for you. You need more room. You know it. You feel it. You also know it's time to move on.

Once again we return to the subject of stress, which has become such a defining way of life for many of us. Always remind yourself that stress is not really about too much. Rather stress is about not enough. Not enough room, not enough time, not enough joy, not enough freedom, not enough choice, not enough money, not enough help, not enough that nurtures you. Stress—whether stress is inflicted on you by some outside stressor or whether you are constricting yourself by your thoughts—contorts you into life spaces that are too small for you. If you feel perpetually stressed-out by life, it's time to get out of the small spaces of your life and create your own life journey from stressed-out to peaceful.

~

QUESTIONS TO THINK ABOUT

1. Do you consider your life as a journey?
2. Do you feel stuck in inertia?
3. How does the inevitability of constant change on Earth provide hope?
4. What is your current phase of life?
5. How do you know if it's time to move on?
6. What do you think you're meant to do?
7. How much of your stressed-out state of mind results from spending the time of your life doing unimportant things that don't matter to you?
8. How can you create your own life journey from stressed-out to peaceful?

About the Author

Dr. Kalinda Rose Stevenson is an award-winning author, whose published writings include both academic and non-academic books. She earned her Ph.D. at the Graduate Theological Union in Berkeley, California, in cooperation with the University of California at Berkeley. She is a former teacher of university and theological seminary students. Most of all, she is a writer who loves to write.

She currently lives with her husband in the Las Vegas area of Nevada, where she writes books, tends to her sometimes neglected websites, works out in the gym, hikes in the desert with camera in hand, and stays out of casinos.

Find out more at:

KalindaRoseStevenson.com

StressedOutToPeaceful.com

Write a Review

If you like the book, please leave an honest review on Amazon. I welcome constructive feedback and would love to hear what you think of the book. I'm especially eager to hear how the book gave you insights to create a peaceful life.

Resources

BOOKS BY KALINDA ROSE STEVENSON

How to Get Out of the True Self Trap: The Life Changing Secret of Heroic Stories.
http://trueselftrap.com
/change-your-life-put-down-your-mirror/

Your True Self Identity: How Familiar Translations of Bible Verses in the Gospel of Matthew Hide Your True Identity From You. Does the Bible Really Say That? Series.
http://doesthebiblesaythat.com/your-true-self-identity/

Gospel of Wealth or Poverty? How Do Bible Verses about Jesus, Wealth, Poverty, and Heaven Affect Your Income? Does the Bible Really Say That? Series.
http://doesthebiblesaythat.com
/gospel-of-wealth-or-poverty-income-inequality/

Book Writing Made Simple 3-in-1: How to Write a Book the Simple Way.
http://bookwritingmadesimple.com/book-writing-3-in-1/

On Writing Words: A Writer's Essential Relations with Words.
http://bookwritingmadesimple.com
/on-writing-words-a-writers-essential-relations-with-words/

Notes

[1] "Pogo" is the title and central character of a long-running daily American comic strip by Walt Kelly. "We have met the enemy and he is us" is one of his best known quotations, first used in an Earth Day poster in 1970. http://www.thisdayinquotes.com/2011/04 /we-have-met-enemy-and-he-is-us.html. Accessed March 8, 2015.

[2] Edward Bulwer-Lytton went down in history for another memorable phrase, "It was a dark and stormy night." Since 1982 the English Department at San Jose State University has sponsored the Bulwer-Lytton Fiction Contest, a whimsical literary competition that challenges entrants to compose the opening sentence to the worst of all possible novels. http://en.wikipedia.org/wiki/Bulwer-Lytton_Fiction_Contest. Accessed March 8, 2015.

[3] Stephen R. Covey. *The Seven Habits of Highly Successful People* (New York: Simon & Schuster, 1989), 287-307.

[4] Scott Thorpe. *How to Think Like Einstein: Simple Ways to Break the Rules and Discover Your Hidden Genius* (New York: Barnes & Noble Books, 2000), 135.

[5] Thorpe 15.

[6] First inauguration of Franklin D. Roosevelt. http://en.wikipedia.org /wiki/First_inauguration_of_Franklin_D._Roosevelt. Accessed March 8, 2015.

[7] "Desiderata." http://allpoetry.com/Desiderata---Words-for-Life.

[8] Linda R. Monk. *The Words We Live By: Your Annotated Guide to the Constitution* (New York: Hyperion, 2003), 127.

[9] You might be wondering about "the hump in the floor." Before automobiles were built with front wheel drive, the hump on the floor of the backseat allowed room for the drive shaft to the rear wheels. I don't know the particular Buick model my father drove, nor do I know the exact height of the hump. I do remember that the hump was several inches high and made sitting in the middle seat very uncomfortable.

[10] Wikipedia. "It's the Great Pumpkin, Charlie Brown." http://en.wikipedia.org /wiki/It%27s_the_Great_Pumpkin,_Charlie_Brown. Accessed March 8, 2015.

[11] Wikipedia. "Helen Keller." http://en.wikipedia.org/wiki/Helen_Keller. Accessed March 8, 2015.

[12] BrainHQ. "What is Brain Plasticity?" http://www.brainhq.com /brain-resources/brain-plasticity/what-is-brain-plasticity. Accessed March 8, 2015.

[13] Heidi Kyser. "High Alert." Desert Companion. https://knpr.org /desert-companion/2014-12/high-alert-taking-care-cops-minds.

Accessed March 8, 2015.

[14] C. S. Lewis. *The Screwtape Letters* (New York: Image Books, 1981), 34.

[15] Wikipedia. "Newton's laws of motion." http://en.wikipedia.org/wiki/Newton%27s_laws_of_motion. Accessed March 8, 2015.

[16] Norman Cousins. *Head First: The Biology of Hope* (New York: E. P. Dutton, 1989), back cover.

[17] Lewis Carroll. *Alice's Adventures in Wonderland* (New York: Dover Publications, 1993), 1. Wikipedia. "White Rabbit." http://en.wikipedia.org/wiki/White_Rabbit. Accessed March 8, 2015.

[18] Rudyard Kipling. "If." Poetry Foundation. http://www.poetryfoundation.org/poem/175772. Accessed March 8, 2015.

[19] "Invisible Gorilla." http://www.theinvisiblegorilla.com /gorilla_experiment.html. Accessed March 8, 2015.

[20] Hal Zina Bennett. *Write from the Heart: Unleashing the Power of Your Creativity* (Novato, CA: Nataraj Publishing, 1995), 108-109.

[21] United States Holocaust Memorial Museum. "The Interior: The Hall of Remembrance." http://www.ushmm.org/information/about-the-museum/architecture-and-art/inside-the-museum-the-hall-of-remembrance. Accessed March 8, 2015.

[22] The Phrase Finder. "The meaning and origin of the expression: Bad hair day." http://www.phrases.org.uk/meanings/bad-hair-day.html. Accessed March 8, 2015.

[23] Wikiquote. "Snow White and the Seven Dwarfs (1937 film)." http://en.wikiquote.org/wiki/Snow_White_and_the_Seven_Dwarfs. Accessed March 8, 2015.

[24] Noah St. John. *Permission to Succeed* (Deerfield Beach, Florida: Health Communications, 1999), 104.

[25] St. John 52.

[26] St. John 104.

[27] Jessica Samakow. "You Are What You Wear: The Dangerous Lessons Kids Learn From Sexist T-Shirts." http://www.huffingtonpost.com/2014/12/03 /dangerous-lessons-from-sexist-shirts_n_6102096.html. Accessed March 8, 2015.

[28] Quote Investigator. "No One Can Make You Feel Inferior Without Your Consent." http://quoteinvestigator.com/2012/04/30/no-one-inferior/. Accessed March 8, 2015.

[29] Wikipedia. "Malala Yousafzai." http://en.wikipedia.org/wiki/Malala_Yousafzai, Accessed March 8, 2015.

[30] Laurene Powell Jobs. "Malala Yousafzai." Forbes December 15, 2014, 70-74.

[31] NBC News. "Teen daughters find strength to lift 3,000-pound NBC tractor off father." April 10, 2013. http://usnews.nbcnews.com/_news/2013/04/10 /17689146-teen-daughters-find-strength-to-lift-3000-pound-tractor-off-father?lite. Accessed March 8, 2015.

32 Marsha Sinetar. *Do What You Love, The Money Will Follow* (New York: Dell Publishing Company, 1990).

33 National Institute of Mental Health. "What is psychotherapy?" http://www.nimh.nih.gov/health/topics/psychotherapies /index.shtml. Accessed March 8, 2015.

34 Quote Investigator. "You Just Chip Away Everything That Doesn't Look Like David." http://quoteinvestigator.com/2014/06/22/chip-away/. Accessed March 8, 2015.

35 James Ryan. *Screenwriting from the Heart: The Technique of the Character-Driven Screenplay* (New York: Billboard Books, 2000), 34.

36 Kalinda Rose Stevenson. *How to Get Out of the True Self Trap: The Life Changing Secret of Heroic Stories* (Las Vegas: ABKA Publishing, 2014), 7.

37 Ryan 35.

38 Thorpe 58.

39 Robert Fritz. *Creating* (New York: Fawcett Columbine, 991), 141.

40 Reinhold Niebuhr. "The Serenity Prayer." SKDesigns. http://skdesigns.com/internet/articles/prose/niebuhr/serenity_prayer/. Accessed March 8, 2015.

41 Mihaly Csikszentmihalyi. *Flow: The Psychology of Optimal Experience* (New York: HarperPerennial, 1990), 4.

42 Read the entire story of "The Ugly Duckling" by Hans Christian Andersen. Originally published in 1844. "The Ugly Duckling." http://hca.gilead.org.il/ugly_duc.html. Accessed March 8, 2015.

43 Csikszentmihalyi 8.

44 Wikipedia. "Newton's laws of motion." http://en.wikipedia.org/wiki/Newtons_laws_of_motion. Accessed March 8, 2015.

45 TeacherTech. "First Law of Motion." Rice University. http://teachertech.rice.edu/Participants/louviere/Newton/law1.html. Accessed March 8, 2015.

46 TeacherTech.

47 Quote Investigator. "Life is What Happens To You While You're Busy Making Other Plans." http://quoteinvestigator.com /2012/05/06/other-plans/. Accessed March 8, 2015.

48 Robert Frost. "The Road Not Taken." Poetry Foundation. http://www.poetryfoundation.org/poem/173536. Accessed March 8, 2015.

49 British spelling is "traveller." American spelling is "traveler." Antonio Machado. "Traveller, There Is No Path." http://minimo.50webs.org/caminante_eng.html. Accessed March 8, 2015.

Index

Because the whole book is about *thinking* and *stress,* the terms *stress, stressed-out, thinking,* and *thought* are not included as primary terms in the index.

A

abundance, 10, 89-90, 92-93, 96-98, 100-101
abuses, 36, 45, 48, 53, 110, 113-15
acceptance, 33, 123, 147, 205-06, 208, 211, 214, 220, 223
accordions, 193-94
actions, 96, 141, 180-81, 195, 198, 201, 228
active doer, 180-81, 201
activities, 79, 83, 85 86, 194-95, 198-99, 202, 209, 216-17, 228-29
acts of consciousness, 200
adrenal cortex, 57
adults, 36, 85, 183, 219
adventure stories, 117
advertising, 78, 93, 135
advice, 60, 122, 174, 176, 210
affirmations, 143
Ahiqar, 28
Alcoholics Anonymous, 205
Alice and Jerry, 119
Alice in Wonderland, 77
analyzing past, 144
Anatomy of an Illness
    Norman Cousins, 70
Andersen, Hans Christian
    The Ugly Duckling, 216
Angelou, Maya, 195
anger, 31, 36-37, 39, 41, 113, 118, 122, 157, 207-08
angles, 67, 69
anguish, 208
anxiety, 27, 31, 36, 209, 220
appearance, 29-30, 133-35, 138

approval, 133, 188, 223-24
Archie Bunker, 52
arms, 119, 206
assumptions, 33-35, 41, 112, 166-67
attitudes, 18, 97-98, 100, 112, 150, 213
awareness, 14, 20, 110, 154

B

babies, 156, 187, 219
bad day, 69, 130
bad hair, 129-30, 135
balance, 192-93, 196
Ballard, David W., 9-10
balloons, 24-26, 145
Bard, Carl, 84, 87
basketball players video, 99-100, 102, 165
Beatty, Melody, 89, 101
Beautiful Boy, 232
beginnings, 174, 185, 230
beliefs, 26, 35, 38, 49-50, 59, 70-72, 78-79, 81, 84, 98, 100, 104, 108, 113, 119, 125, 135, 140, 146-47, 149, 153-54, 161, 172, 198, 200, 212-13, 218, 223-25, 230-31
believing, 61, 64-65, 71, 81, 100-01, 107-08, 115, 117, 125, 129, 131-32, 138, 140, 143, 151, 160, 167, 172, 178, 183, 211, 224
Bennett, Hal Zina, 107
Big Bang, 192
blessings, 200-201
blood, 133, 152, 193
boa constrictor, 23

bodies, 12, 23-24, 50, 67, 106-07, 114, 194, 217-18, 220
brain, 56-59, 61, 63, 65, 97, 106, 114, 241
Buckingham, Marcus, 85, 87, 183
Buffy the Vampire Slayer, 129
bullies, 11, 45, 47, 50, 151
Bulwer-Lytton, Edward, 28, 241
Bündchen, Gisele, 159
busyness, 110, 78-79, 82, 150, 198, 202, 219, 231
butterflies, 173-76, 178

C

calling, 29, 137, 231
calmness, 206, 209-10, 213-14
car trips, 47
Carnegie, Dale, 70
Carroll, Lewis
    Alice's Adventures in
        Wonderland, 77, 242
catastrophes, 9-10, 36, 149, 210, 218, 232
caterpillars, 173-76, 178
cerebrum, 57
characters, 168, 170
childhood, 47, 91, 119, 140
children, 9, 16, 25, 36, 48, 53, 59, 82, 85, 109, 119, 140, 150, 152-53, 155, 172, 180-82, 206, 218-19, 230
Chopra, Deepak, 103, 105
Christmas, 32-33
chronic stress, 9-11, 18, 21, 36, 41, 58-59
clocks, 79, 83, 121
clothing, 133
cocoons, 173, 174, 175, 176
combat veterans, 106
communicating, 49, 157
communications, 81, 157
comparing, 82, 101, 131, 133, 139, 142, 145-47, 149
compassion, 20, 106, 112, 115, 125-26, 212
competitions, 131, 138, 147, 241
complainers, 196-97
complaining, 15, 46, 48, 50, 52, 101, 145, 196-98, 201-02, 206

complaints, 83, 101, 197
compression, 48, 97-98, 185, 193-95, 218
    expansion and contraction, 193-94
computers, 83, 95, 124
confidence, 149-51, 161
conflicts, 27, 95, 122, 209, 213
consequences, 47, 52
constant changes, 63, 185, 229-30, 235
constriction, 23-25, 46, 56, 97, 100, 122, 208, 235
contexts, 18-19, 35-36, 105
conversations, 48, 80, 136, 176
Coolidge, Calvin, 234
cortisol, 57-58
cosmic self, 212
costs, 46, 51, 72, 79, 83, 86, 96, 200
courage, 39, 53, 153-54, 205, 212
Cousins, Norman, 71
    Anatomy of an Illness, 70, 73, 242
    Head First, 70, 73, 242
Covey, Stephen R., 28, 241
    The Seven Habits of Highly
        Successful People, 28, 241
creating, 12, 29, 31-33, 39, 41, 58, 97, 107, 141, 147, 155, 165-66, 169-72, 174-77, 183-88, 205, 209, 234-35
Creating
    Robert Fritz, 186
creations, 96, 172-76, 181-82, 184-85, 187-89, 195
creative process, 174, 184, 191, 194
creativity, 27, 53, 231
creators, 12, 144, 170, 177, 179, 181-82, 184-85, 187-88
Csikszentmihalyi, Mihaly
    Flow, 212, 217, 243

D

daily life, 9-10, 48, 150, 156-57
dangers, 39

decisions, 14, 40, 62, 69, 86, 96-97, 104, 106, 109, 145, 150-51, 156, 160-61, 170, 176, 210-11
demands, 46-48, 78
Desiderata, 39, 241
desires, 46, 93, 96, 152, 154-55, 157, 160, 165, 172, 176-78, 187, 189, 201, 208, 214, 231
detachment, 67, 69
determination, 201
direct object, 180-81, 189
discovering, 142, 153, 167, 169-71, 218-19, 230
Disraeli, Benjamin, 212
distance, 14, 49, 62, 69, 78, 83, 188
distorting, 68
distortions, 25, 68
distrust, 157
draining, 196, 202
dreams, 46, 50, 53, 55, 79, 135, 140, 146, 151, 154, 160-61, 170, 172, 177, 182-83, 189, 234
driving crazy, 50-51
ducks, 218-19, 222, 224
Dyer, Wayne, 31
dynamic energy, 170-71, 193-95

E

Earth, 10-11, 62-63, 70, 84, 147, 156, 170-71, 192, 229, 235, 241
Eastern philosophical traditions, 112, 193
easy, 216
egg stage, 173
eggs121, 123, 173, 175-76
eggshells, 48, 157
Ehrmann, Max, 39
Eiffel Tower, 68
Einstein, Albert, 33, 67, 152, 172, 184, 191-92, 228
elephant in the living room, 49
Ellis, Havelock, 120, 222
emotions, 14, 28, 36, 71-72, 90, 104-05, 113-14, 187, 198
encouragement, 177
endings, 84, 87, 230

ends, 28, 81, 83, 90-91, 102, 142, 145, 158, 192, 206, 213, 227, 231
energizing, 195-96, 198-02
energy, 46, 63, 121, 188, 191-92, 195-200, 202
Epicurus, 92, 98, 102
essential wounds, 107-08, 116
Evil Queen, 131
evolution, 171

F

failures, 78, 144
families, 31-32, 47, 49, 59, 86, 110, 137, 177, 200, 209
fat shaming, 134
father, 51, 119, 153-55, 241-42
fears, 37-39, 49, 59, 104, 106, 110, 113, 118, 131, 185
feelings, 9-10, 12-14, 16, 19-20, 31-33, 37, 41, 49, 51-52, 67-70, 83, 85, 90, 96-98, 101-02, 132, 150, 156, 158, 165-66, 185, 196, 201, 209, 213, 218, 229-30, 232, 234
Ferris wheels, 47, 51, 62-63, 241
finding, 105, 169
fireworks, 14-17, 21, 206
First Amendment, 45
floating, 206
flow, 121-22, 216-17, 222, 231
Flow
    The Psychology of Optimal Experience
        Mihaly Csikszentmihalyi, 217, 243
focus, 10, 12, 18, 39, 70, 80-81, 96-98, 144-45, 175, 185, 187, 189, 191, 195-96
fog, 15-17, 206
forces, 12, 23-26, 36, 62, 69, 71, 73, 108, 146, 192-93, 197, 207, 228-29
forgetting, 17, 111, 120-23, 144
Form, 167
foundations, 174
Fourth of July, 14, 15, 16
fragmentation, 119, 219
fragments, 56

freedom, 45-46, 53-54, 160, 218, 234
Freud, Sigmund, 144
Freudian psychoanalysis, 144
Fritz, Robert, 186, 243
    Creating, 11, 19, 141, 163, 165-66, 169, 172, 174, 186-87, 243
Frost, Robert, 233, 243
frustrations, 52, 81, 201, 207
future, 56, 64-65, 73, 113, 117, 119-20, 124-25, 144, 182, 185, 224
future shock, 94
Future Shock
    Alvin Toffler, 94

G

game, 39, 59, 85, 142, 147
Gandhi, Mahatma, 152
Gaynor, Gloria, 139
girls, 52, 134, 154
goals, 60, 146, 191
good news, 10, 12, 59, 230
gorilla, 99-100, 102, 242
gossip, 51-52, 54
grabbing, 78, 118-19
grace, 130, 158, 205, 215-17, 220-24
gratitude, 89, 97-98, 100-02, 215
Great Pumpkin, 50, 241
Greek philosophical ideas, 167
Gretzky, Wayne, 160
Groundhog Day, 64
guilt, 79, 185

H

habits, 28, 137, 177, 197
habitual language, 29
hair, 129-30, 133, 135, 242
hammer, 94
Hanh, Thich Nhat, 104-05
harm, 112-14, 116
Harry Potter, 49
hawks, 68-69
Hazlitt, William, 215, 221
Head First, The Biology of Hope
    Norman Cousins, 71, 242
healing, 58, 112, 122, 126, 221-22

health, 27
hearts, 87, 107, 193-94
helplessness, 58, 59, 65, 106, 150, 185
Hill, Napoleon, 95
    Think and Grow Rich, 95
Hoffer, Eric, 158
holding, 104, 117, 119, 123, 222
holidays, 31-32
Holocaust Memorial, 121, 242
Hooks, Bell, 107
hopes, 15, 70-73, 119
How to Think Like Einstein
    Scott Thorpe, 33, 241
human, 10, 45, 61, 71, 80, 86, 93, 107, 120, 155, 165, 167, 173, 183, 212
hump in the floor, 47, 241
Humpty Dumpty, 121, 123
hurts, 58

I

ice skaters, 216
ideal plane, 167
identities, 58, 81, 106, 124-26, 131, 168, 170, 178, 217-23
If
    Rudyard Kipling, 78-79
illnesses, 10, 70-71, 166
illusions, 80, 112, 125
images, 13, 38, 56-57, 78, 104-05, 119, 125, 129, 133-34
imagining, 39, 56, 60, 119-20, 124-25, 137, 145, 152, 155, 182, 184, 213
imbalance, 46, 90
impatience, 77, 83
Indiana Jones-type hero, 117
inertia, 177, 227-29, 231, 235
inferior feelings, 141-42, 147
insanity, 33
insights, 11, 58, 84, 151, 159, 175, 209, 213, 218, 221, 231-32
intentions, 146-47, 200-01, 213
internet, 10, 133, 243
intuitions, 158-59, 232
inventory, 156

J

James, William, 23, 26
Jampolsky, Gerald, 12-13, 17-18, 20
jealousy, 131, 146
Jones, Suzanne, 149, 151
journeys, 168, 177, 220, 227, 229-30, 233-35
joy, 227, 52, 84-86, 157, 222, 234
judging, 20, 79, 133, 145

K

Kabat-Zinn, Jon, 223
Keane, Bil, 77
Keller, Gary, 80
Keller, Helen, 55, 241
Kelly, Walt, 11, 241
kindness, 10, 20, 23, 38-39, 51, 64, 79, 82, 85, 92, 100, 110, 112, 133, 137, 143, 145, 154-55, 159, 165, 168, 173-74, 187, 195, 197, 200, 202, 221
King, Martin Luther, 55
King, Stephen, 158
Kingma, Daphne Rose, 117, 119
Kipling, Rudyard, 78, 242
   If, 78, 242
Know Yourself, 167
knowing difference, 62, 80, 181, 207, 209
Kornfield, Jack, 104-05

L

lack, 55, 91-93, 97, 100-01, 106, 150-51, 158, 185, 217, 228-29
larva stage, 173
late, 49, 59, 77-78, 197, 219
laundry, 9, 61, 150
Law of Inertia, 228
Law of Undulation, 61-62
Laws of Motion, 61, 228, 242-43
Le Guin, Ursula K., 227
legs, 47, 229
Lembo, John, 136
Lennon, John, 232
lessons, 207, 211-12

letting go, 103-13, 115-24, 126, 222-23, 225
Lewis, C. S., 61, 242
   The Screwtape Letters, 61, 242
liberation, 224
lifetime, 59, 106, 140, 154
light, 70, 193
limitations, 91, 101
lists, 31, 78, 105, 150, 156, 219
lives, 9, 13, 19-20, 24, 27, 36, 64, 79-80, 103, 116, 122-23, 151, 156, 172, 189, 192, 219, 222
living beings, 26, 171
love, 27, 33, 86-87, 111, 119, 131, 140, 154, 157, 159-60, 175, 182-89, 195, 198, 201
Loving Mirrors, 132
lying, 158

M

Machado, Antonio, 233, 243
making do, 91-92
Marsha Sinetar, 159, 243
   Do What You Love, The Money Will Follow, 159, 243
material world, 167
measuring, 132-33
Meir, Golda, 155
members, 123
memorials, 120-21
memories, 17, 105-06, 110-11, 115-16, 120-23, 125, 155, 185-86
men, 15, 48, 52-53, 121, 133-35
mental disorder, 166, 168
metamorphosis, 173, 175, 178, 223
metaphors, 51, 61-63, 118-19, 132, 168
Michelangelo
   statue of David, 168
military, 58, 209
minds, 12-13, 17, 20, 29, 38, 49, 53, 55, 57, 72, 86, 90, 100, 103, 106, 110, 116, 129, 143, 154, 172, 184, 186, 209-13, 216, 219-20, 232-33, 235
mindsets
   changing, 19, 188, 218

different, 229
intending the best, 146
lack, 91, 101
right, 89
mingling, 120, 223
minor matters, 96, 102
minutes, 78-79, 83
mirroring process, 132, 141
mirrors, 130, 132, 138
money, 14, 79, 90, 92, 96-97, 102,
150, 159, 234
moods, 18, 197, 199
Morrissey, Mary Manin, 103, 105
Mortensen, Viggo, 210
motions, 53, 83, 192-93, 196, 216-
17, 220, 222, 228
movements, 61, 63, 194, 210, 217,
228
moving, 19, 62, 64, 84, 99, 103-04,
116, 120-21, 123, 191, 216, 227-
29, 231, 234
moving walkway, 116, 227, 229
multiswitching, 80-81
multitasking, 80, 87

N

National Institute of Mental Health,
166, 243
Negative Reflection, 132
New Age, 89, 112, 211
new rich, 92
Newton, Isaac, 61, 228, 242-43
Niebuhr, Reinhold, 205, 243
Serenity Prayer, 205, 243
Norville, Deborah, 100
nouveau riche, 92

O

O'Nan, Stewart, 123
observing, 67, 69
old money, 92
on the go, 78, 81
opinions, 132-33, 136, 138-39, 141,
145, 174-75
opposable thumbs, 192
opposing and complementary
forces, 192-95
oppression, 46, 53

options, 17, 40, 59, 93-94, 96, 124
orbits, 70, 192

P

pains, 10, 48-49, 54, 58, 103-04,
107-08, 116, 122, 126, 221
parents, 24, 153-54, 187
parts, 11, 25, 106-07, 115, 122-24,
168-71, 199, 217, 220-23, 231
passion, 185, 188, 195-96, 198,
231
past, 19, 65, 71, 77, 89, 101, 103-
05, 109-11, 114, 116-20, 123,
125-26, 144, 185-86, 188, 222
path, 176, 206, 230, 233
peace, 12, 17-19, 27-28, 32, 34,
56, 72-73, 85, 89-91, 101-02,
119-20, 139, 172, 177, 184, 186,
191, 200, 202, 208-09, 211, 213,
224, 238
pen, 28, 104, 106, 110
perceptions, 18, 51, 68, 77, 90, 92,
98, 100, 102, 107-08, 112, 129,
132, 135, 139, 145, 147, 149,
159, 186, 219, 225
permission, 132, 146
Permission to Succeed, 132, 141,
242
Noah St. John, 132, 141, 242
persistence, 176, 234
person, 186-89
perspectives, 18, 61, 67-70, 72-73,
78, 81, 85, 91, 101, 113, 142,
146, 185-89, 208, 216, 220-21,
224
phases, 227, 230, 235
physics textbooks, 61, 228
pianist, 160
pictures, 13, 56, 68-70, 86, 95, 107,
119
plastic, 56-57, 59, 107
Platonic influence, 167
playing, 59, 85, 96, 194
Pogo cartoon, 11
possibilities, 32, 37-38, 41, 57, 59-
60, 69, 104, 119, 125, 144, 155,
170-71, 184, 220
post-traumatic stress disorder
(PTSD), 58-59, 106

power, 13-14, 16, 19, 29, 45-46,
    48-49, 51-53, 58, 63, 69, 96, 98,
    105, 125, 136, 145, 151-52, 171,
    185, 191, 193, 195-96, 198, 212,
    217, 222
practice, 134, 136, 160, 217
prayer, 101, 205, 243
preferences, 104-08
present, 55, 60, 65, 77, 81, 144,
    186, 200, 211, 213, 223
pressures, 24-25, 94
problems, 9, 33, 52, 67-68, 72, 129,
    135, 144, 147, 151, 165-66, 168-
    70, 172, 177-78, 181-85, 188,
    207, 211, 221, 234
psychopaths and sociopaths, 158
psychotherapy, 144, 166-67
pupal stage, 175
putting together, 116, 123, 222

Q

quality of life, 27, 78, 184
quests, 169-70, 223, 230, 239

R

Real You, 112, 167-68, 171
recreating, 172
re-creation, 176
reflections, 219
relationships, 9, 72, 77, 79-80, 82-
    83, 87, 122, 130, 157-58, 213,
    230
relieving stress, 11
remembering, 52, 70, 97-99, 110,
    120-21, 123, 125-26, 160, 184,
    187, 221, 231
Remembrance Hall, 121
resignation, 53, 208
resistance, 23-24, 30, 104-05, 107-
    11, 113, 119, 123, 208resisting,
    107-09, 116
responsibilities, 9, 86, 90, 150, 183,
    185, 211
road less traveled by, 233
Road Not Taken, The
    Robert Frost, 233, 243
Rohn, Jim, 143
room, 100, 218, 234

Roosevelt, Eleanor, 141-42
Roosevelt, Franklin D., 38, 241
rules, 23, 33-34, 53
rushing, 77-78, 81
Russell, Bertrand, 84
Ryan, James
    Screenwriting from the Heart,
        168, 170, 243

S

sadness, 49, 122
San Francisco, 14-16, 21, 135,
    174-75, 206
Saramago, José, 103
Saunders, Allen, 232
saying, 14, 28, 34, 39, 48-51, 53-
    54, 77, 111, 136-37, 142, 157,
    159, 172, 212
saying out loud, 46, 49-51
Sayles, Ginie, 174, 176
scarcity, 91, 97
scars, 106, 107, 111
schedules, 78, 86, 231
screenwriting, 175
Screenwriting from the Heart
    James Ryan, 168, 243
Screwtape Letters, The
    C. S. Lewis, 61, 242
seconds, 11, 78, 83
secrets, 46, 49
self, 121, 132, 136, 138, 212, 231
self-appreciation, 145
self-awareness, 219
self-betrayal, 115
self-criticism, 144, 145
self-esteem, 139-40, 143, 145
self-help, 143, 166-68, 219
self-help teachers, 13, 105, 143
self-image, 129-32, 134, 138-40,
    145, 149
self-induced stress, 16, 39, 50, 210
self-perceptions, 18, 145, 149
self-talk, 136-38
self-trust, 37, 149-51, 153-55, 157-
    59, 232
separating, 121, 123, 222
serenity, 72-73, 205-11, 213-14,
    243
Serenity Prayer

Reinhold Niebuhr, 205, 243
setbacks, 192
Seven Habits of Highly Successful
  People, The
  Covey, Stephen R., 28, 241
shalom, 213
shapes, 23-25, 35, 56, 173, 175-76
sharpening the saw, 28-29
Shaw, George Bernard, 165, 169
Shawshank Redemption, The, 124
shyness, 48
sickness, 27
silence, 45-50
skills, 14, 27, 146, 156, 160
Snow White and the Seven
  Dwarfs, 130, 242
spaces, 56, 200, 218, 234-35
speaking, 14, 28, 45-46, 48, 52, 54,
  152, 157
speech, 45-46, 50-51, 53-54, 59,
  105, 141, 208
Spender, Dale, 179
spirit, 39, 50, 52, 71, 104, 183, 231,
  234
Spock, Benjamin, 156
squeezing, 23-24, 26, 48, 98, 194
St. John, Noah, 132, 141, 242
  Permission to Succeed, 132,
  141, 242
stagnation, 231
steroid hormone, 57
strains, 25-26
Stressed-Out Off Switch, 11-12
stressed-out season, 31, 33
stressors, 11-13, 24-29, 48-51, 58-
  59, 68-69, 72, 77, 106, 130, 149-
  50, 181, 183, 205, 209, 230
subject, 179-81, 234
substitutes, 39, 50, 61, 90, 165
success, 97, 135, 143-44, 146-47,
  160, 174-76, 191
suffering, 48, 53, 58, 104-08, 112,
  115, 123, 208, 222-23
suicide, 49
Sun, 63, 70, 192, 229
survival, 46, 97
swans, 216, 219
Sweetland, Ben, 89
swords, 28, 40
syntax, 179, 181

T

taking personally, 69, 213-14
talents, 133, 142, 146-47, 153
talk therapy, 166
talking, 31, 46, 49-50, 52, 67, 137,
  177
telephones, 80, 95
telling, 51-53, 59, 78, 143, 153
Temple of Apollo at Delphi, 167
thankfulness, 98, 101
things, 205, 207-08, 211, 213-14
Think and Grow Rich
  Napoleon Hill, 95
Thorpe, Scott
  How to Think Like Einstein, 33,
  241
threats, 9, 38-39, 46, 48, 57, 149
time, 20, 63-64, 77-87, 95, 170,
  175-76, 183, 185, 197, 219, 228,
  231-32, 234-35
times, 70, 72, 155
Toffler, Alvin
  Future Shock, 94
too little, 85, 87, 90, 92, 98, 102,
  131, 183
tools, 27-29, 94-95, 158, 166, 181
tourists, 230
Tracy, Brian, 129
transformations, 173, 218
transforming, 20, 28, 173
traumas, 9, 18-19, 36, 41, 58, 105-
  06, 108, 110-11, 113-16, 119,
  121-26, 160, 205, 221-22
True Self, 166-71, 177
trust, 150-51, 153-61, 207
truth, 49, 52, 57, 143, 145, 147,
  150, 153, 157
Tutu, Desmond, 70
Twain, Mark, 15
twenty-first century, 11, 94-95
twenty-four hours, 80, 82-83
types of stress, 9-10, 19, 25, 149-
  50

U

ugly duckling, 218- 22
Ugly Duckling, The

Hans Christian Andersen, 216, 243
undulations, 61, 64
unique experiences, 17, 19
unique lives, 147
United States Constitution, 45
universe, 63, 107, 187, 212
untrue assessments, 69
ups and downs, 62
upsetting, 69, 142, 147, 207
user experience, 94

V

validity, 68, 172
values, 106, 113-16, 123, 125-26, 140, 146, 149, 159
valuing, 133, 146
vantage points, 67, 135
victims, 12, 23, 29, 181, 184
virtues, 149, 151, 215
vision, 19, 55-56, 60, 67-68, 70, 89, 101, 119, 121, 124-26, 170, 172, 177-78, 182, 184-85, 201, 219, 220, 221, 222, 224
vision., 68
visionaries, 55, 57, 184
visions, 70, 119, 182, 219-21
vocabulary, 29, 39, 60, 181

W

Waitley, Denis, 144
Walker, Alice, 45
wars, 27-28, 36, 91, 106, 120, 209, 213, 220
watching, 60, 67, 109, 118
way of life, 9-10, 19, 94, 150, 234
way out, 19, 56, 65
wealth, 92, 95, 98, 100, 160, 239
weapons, 23, 26-27, 29, 100, 110
Weil, Simone, 207
wellbeing, 85, 200, 201, 213
Western cultures, 167
what happens, 46, 110

what matters, 46, 96-97, 102, 232
what you love, 87, 159-60, 183-84, 188-89, 195, 201
White Rabbit, 77, 242
Whitehead, Alfred North, 34-35
wholeness, 19-20, 67-68, 116, 119, 122-23, 125, 213, 220-25
Williams, Robin, 49
Winfrey, Oprah, 91, 191, 195
wisdom, 20, 33, 49, 61, 87, 104, 120, 144, 160, 174, 176, 192, 205, 207, 210-12
women, 31-32, 48, 52-53, 82, 133-135, 155, 232
words, 145
work, 29, 57, 62, 80, 82-86, 89-90, 103, 107, 131, 140, 142, 150, 154, 156, 172, 174-75, 183, 19496, 197, 199, 201, 216-17, 219, 230
world, 9-10, 18-19, 28, 31, 36, 38-39, 49, 55, 70, 77, 81-82, 89, 94, 107-8, 115, 122-24, 131, 135-36, 144, 146, 147, 151, 154-55, 158, 165, 171, 176, 181-82, 189, 198, 200, 202, 207, 211, 213, 224, 228, 234
worrying, 27, 38, 134, 157, 210, 213, 216
wounds, 107, 111, 113, 115-16, 122, 222

Y

years, 11, 15, 63, 71, 99, 119, 144, 182, 217, 229
Yin and yang, 193
Yousafzai, Malala, 152-54, 242

Z

Ziglar, Zig, 97-8, 159

www.ingramcontent.com/pod-product-compliance
Lightning Source LLC
LaVergne TN
LVHW051500080426
835509LV00017B/1846